Quest *for the* Cup

The Detroit Red Wings' Unforgettable Journey to the 1997 Stanley Cup

*By Cynthia Lambert, Bob Wojnowski, Joe Falls, Jerry Green
and The Detroit News Sports Staff*

Edited by Mike Bynum

The Detroit News

GANNETT

The Detroit News

MARK SILVERMAN, *Publisher and Editor*

CHRISTINA BRADFORD, *Managing Editor*

FRANK LOVINSKI, *Deputy Managing Editor*

PHIL LACIURA, *Executive Sports Editor*

ALAN WHITT, *Deputy Sports Editor*

ROB ALLSTETTER, *Deputy Sports Editor*

CHRISTOPHER KOZLOWSKI, *Assistant Managing Editor-Design/Graphics*

DAVID KORDALSKI, *Design/Graphics Editor*

STEVEN FECHT, *Director of Photography*

Acknowledgements

RESEARCH ASSISTANCE
Mike Katz, Chris Farina, Karen Van Antwerp
and Terry Jacoby.

Chapters 4, 5, 6 and 7 reprinted by permission
of *The Detroit News*. Copyright© 1997 by *The
Detroit News*. All rights reserved.

ISBN 1-57243-257-8

COVER DESIGN
Christopher Kozlowski.

BOOK DESIGN
Christopher Kozlowski, David Kordalski,
Dan Janke and Richard Epps.

GRAPHICS
Darryl Swint, Tim Summers and Satoshi
Toyoshima.

PHOTO EDITING
Michael Brown and Jan Lovell.

Published for *The Detroit News* by:
Triumph Books
644 South Clark Steet
Chicago, Illinois 60605
(312) 939-3330

Contents

Heaven *in* Hockeytown

A million fans gathered at Hart Plaza to celebrate the victory.

Sergei
Fedorov

Steve Yzerman with the Cup.

The view from Canada: The Wings' parade down Woodward Ave. ended at Hart Plaza.

Vladimir Konstantinov drinks from the Stanley Cup: "I'm so happy and this tastes so sweet."

Savoring *the* Cup

"I KNOW IN MY HEART MY DAD IS UP THERE HELPING HIS BELOVED Wings bring home the Stanley Cup! He never gave up on them."

That e-mail message from Connie Littman of Shelby Township, Mich., demonstrates why this state has gone slightly bonkers over the Wings' Stanley Cup victory.

Hockey fans always have been known for their loyalty. And few have suffered more from generation to generation than those in Michigan.

It wasn't only because the team had not won the Cup since 1955. It was the way it lost. It was the 16 out of 17 losing seasons from 1970-71 through 1985-86. It was the lack of hope.

That changed dramatically in 1986 when owner Mike Ilitch, who desired a Cup as much as his long-suffering fans, hired Jacques Demers as coach. Demers quickly named Steve Yzerman the youngest captain in franchise history.

The team was suddenly competitive, but the frustration continued.

After two exhilarating trips to the conference finals, Demers was fired after missing the playoffs.

Bryan Murray took over, but the Wings faltered in the playoffs in the same manner his teams in Washington did.

Murray became general manager in 1994, and Scotty Bowman, winner of six Stanley Cups, was hired as coach to end the frustration. It only grew. Bowman and Murray bickered, the Wings failed to land a top goalie for the playoffs and were shockingly ousted by San Jose.

Murray was fired. Bowman traded for Mike Vernon and led the team to the Cup Finals in 1995. But New Jersey won in a sweep. The next year, the Wings won an NHL-record 62 regular-season games, but were no match for Colorado in the Western Conference finals.

Everything about the 1996-97 season was magical. The Wings made a big trade, landing Brendan Shanahan from Hartford. Darren McCarty beat up the Wings' nemesis, Claude Lemieux of Colorado. The Wings humbled the Avalanche in the Western Conference finals and swept the Flyers behind Yzerman and Vernon. Bowman was a genius again.

Throughout the roller-coaster ride of the franchise, *The Detroit News* has been there.

We, too, have history. Joe Falls has been a sports writer for 50 years. Jerry Green has as many memories from Olympia as he does from The Joe.

Their writing helped give perspective to the rest of our coverage.

It was a team effort. Cynthia Lambert, the Wings' beat reporter since 1986, worked tirelessly. Nicknamed "The Shadow" by the Wings because she is always around the team, she had fewer off days during the season than many Wings players. And, like Vernon, she also had support.

Columnist Bob Wojnowski wrote extensively about the Wings and was credited with convincing the team to sign free-agent Joe Kocur, who had been playing in a local beer league.

Columnist Terry Foster, an NBA and NFL expert, proved his versatili-ty. John Niyo wrote outstanding features and stories all season as Lambert's backup. John U. Bacon provided in-depth features. The rest of the coverage included great work from Dave Dye, Dave Goricki, Ted Kulfan, Vartan Kupelian and others.

The photo department, under the direction of Steve Fecht, produced quality work on a daily basis.

The design and graphics department, under the leadership of Chris Kozlowski and David Kordalski, showed why it is annually recognized as one of the nation's best.

And then there is our version of The Grind Line. Our copy desk and inside managers who on many game nights started work at 4 p.m. and didn't leave the building until 6 a.m. They are: Rob Allstetter, Jeff Barr, Art Brooks, Bev Eckman, Rick Epps, Brian Handley, Terry Jacoby, Dan Janke, Darryl Swint, Robert Jones, Michael Katz, Matt Rennie, Duke Ritenhouse, Jim Russ, Jeff Samoray, David Srinivasan, Jim Thompson, Alan Whitt, Steve Wilson and Craig Yuhas.

This book, much like the success of the Wings, was a team effort.

I hope you enjoy it.

Phil Laciura
Executive Sports Editor
The Detroit News

Journey to Greatness

The Red Wings' quest for the Cup

BY BOB WOJNOWSKI

The Detroit News

In a dark, dingy dressing room in the New Jersey swamplands, it took root. It was planted in the hearts and psyches of dejected players, some with eyes red, some with heads down, all suffering from abject humiliation. Out on the ice, the New Jersey Devils celebrated, and as player after player hoisted the Stanley Cup, the cheers thundered.

Through thick concrete walls, the Red Wings could hear the noise, muffled but so clear, close but so distant. Every now and then, someone, a player, a fan, would run past the open door and let out a whoop that would echo around the room, where players sat, staring at the floor.

Down a hallway, Steve Yzerman, dressed in gray, leaned heavily against a wall. It was an all-too familiar pose, and he offered an all-too familiar response.

"It's just hard to watch someone celebrate at your expense," he said. "You know what I was thinking all during the third period, when all that excitement was building? I kept wishing I was in their shoes."

For 42 years, it was that way, another season gone, another summer spent coveting the other guy's footwear, and hardware. It was late June 1995, and the Wings, heavily favored, were swept in the Stanley Cup Finals by New Jersey. After a 5-2 loss in Game 3, Scotty Bowman had

---

The Red Wings suffered two years of abuse after losing to New Jersey in the 1995 Stanley Cup Finals.

called it "an embarrassment to the National Hockey League."

Game 4 was not much better, another 5-2 loss. Mike Vernon had allowed soft goals as his defense crumbled around him. The Wings, unfamiliar with the Devils' trapping defense, had panicked, had abandoned all team concepts. Bowman failed to inspire them and no player stepped up and led.

In the dressing room, Darren McCarty was in tears. Kris Draper stared straight ahead.

"To walk down the line and shake (the Devils') hands, you see the tears of joy in their eyes, and you realize how precious it is to win the Cup," Draper said. "We have to look at it as a learning experience. You feel for the older guys who might never have this opportunity again."

A hunger must start somewhere, usually in the most profound emptiness. And really, this is where it began, sown in the ultimate failure. To understand how the 1996-97 Red Wings became Stanley Cup champions, to know why Yzerman finally took that long-awaited skate, you must know what drove them, what taught them, who led them.

Three people stand out — the captain, the coach, the goalie.

Bowman was the one with the blueprint, with six Stanley Cup rings. In his first season in Detroit, the top-seeded Wings were shocked in the first round by San Jose. In a sense, Bowman had given them the rope and let them use it as they wished. When the Wings abandoned the defensive plan, the Sharks completed the upset, and Bowman had their attention.

He demanded defense and commanded respect, and beginning with the Jersey failure, he seized power

Vladimir Konstantinov's rugged defensive play would be one of the keys in the Red Wings' return to the Stanley Cup Finals.

and stamped his imprint on the team. He was dictatorial, and at times, players and management resisted. But Bowman was driven by history, by the chance to become the first coach to win Cups with three different franchises, to take his place in NHL lore and deliver on Mike Ilitch's mandate.

Vernon, the goalie, was driven by something more personal. He had been booed out of Calgary, even after leading the Flames to the 1989 Cup. He came to Detroit with a bit of a chip, and when he shouldered much

of the blame for the Jersey debacle, his resolve grew.

Yzerman was the one who adjusted the most, and after an uneasy 1995 summer, he arrived at the start of the following season unsure of his future. Bowman had decided not to make significant changes, but now as the season dawned, rumors swirled that he was shopping Yzerman around the league. Ottawa, Yzerman's hometown, was interested.

This was Bowman's dangerous time, and a critical juncture for the franchise. Operating with deliberate calculation, he contemplated whether to trade Yzerman, whether the move was necessary to alter the makeup of the team, whether the Wings could win with Yzerman as their leader. He contemplated it all ... until Opening Night 1995.

That's when the fans spoke, and everyone listened. When announcer Bud Lynch introduced Yzerman before the game, the applause shook the building ... the fans stood ... Yzerman nodded uncomfortably ... and in a bit of comic relief, Bowman waved to the crowd and ducked from the bench down a tunnel, as if to say, "I'll leave if you don't like me."

It wasn't necessary for Bowman to leave, only for him to understand. The mandate was this: Win a Cup, but do it with the captain. Trade rumors died, and from that point, Bowman and Yzerman seemed more willing to work together, to understand each other. If the Wings were to win a title, they needed the coach, the captain and the goalie, and as they headed into the 1995-96 season, they still had so much to learn.

Championship teams generally take three steps. The first is Foundation-Building, and the Wings constructed theirs in the early 1990's. The second is Learning at the Highest Level, and the Wings were now deep into the process, headed toward the third step — Final Refining.

History is a wonderful teacher. So is failure. The Wings knew their history, were reminded of the franchise's 1955 collar constantly, and they had known failure. They had been regular-season wizards that lacked stamina, strength or the will to win it all, so in an astounding effort, they set out to prove everybody wrong.

Trouble was, they set out too

quickly, as if trying to win the Stanley Cup in January. Their 62 victories were an NHL record, a picture of joyless resolve. Nothing could satiate them, nothing could stop them, nothing but their own obsession.

This was Bowman's biggest mistake. He constructed such an efficient team, it had no idea how to react when adversity struck in the playoffs. The Wings lulled themselves into false security, and spent far too much energy chasing the regular-season record.

By the trading deadline, the Wings were so dominant, Bowman couldn't bring himself to pull the trigger to make them bigger and stronger, an old mantra that had been buried under the tide of success. The only significant moves were to acquire Igor Larionov for Ray Sheppard, and Kirk Maltby for youngster Dan McGillis. Both deals would pay dividends during the regular season but not in the playoffs, not yet.

And for everything they accomplished, the Wings entered the playoffs without a clear-cut No. 1 goalie. Osgood started 50 games, Vernon 32. Both played well, and they shared the Jennings Trophy for fewest goals allowed. But it was difficult to tell if they were that good, or Detroit's defense was that disciplined. Like most of the Wings, neither goalie had faced a major test, and now the playoffs beckoned.

As the Wings prepared to meet Winnipeg in the first round of the 1995-96 season, they were wearing that familiar burden of heavy favorites, and didn't seem to mind.

"It's just the way sports is, why get all tense about it?" Darren McCarty said. "It'd be tough to

accept if we felt we're overachievers. We know we have to win it. If we didn't think we could, that'd be pressure. Maybe we're putting a lot of pressure on ourselves, but we are having fun."

He said it almost like he had to convince himself. Yes, winning was fun for the Wings. But Bowman drove them ruthlessly, and when Winnipeg goalie Nikolai Khabibulin began to make huge saves, the Wings were like spelling bee whizzes suddenly drawing tougher words than they anticipated.

The Jets extended the Wings to six games, and after a clumsy goalie rotation, Bowman settled on Osgood. Then came St. Louis, and trouble — Lesson No. 2 in overconfidence. After the Wings won the first two games and made superstars Wayne Gretzky and Brett Hull look gray and frayed, they couldn't finish as quickly as they needed to.

Game 3 in St. Louis went to overtime, where Keith Primeau misfired on a breakaway moments before the Blues scored the winner. Instead of a possible sweep, the Wings were extended, and energy was drained. St. Louis won three straight before the Wings won a gut check Game 6. Then, back in Detroit, in the second overtime of a scoreless Game 7, Yzerman delivered a slice of magic (an omen?), a 55-foot slap shot that beat Jon Casey and catapulted the Wings to the conference finals. It was the biggest moment of the Captain's career, more important than we realized at the time.

Think about this. If Yzerman doesn't score that goal, if the Wings don't win that game, everything is altered. If they'd been eliminated in round two, Bowman might not have

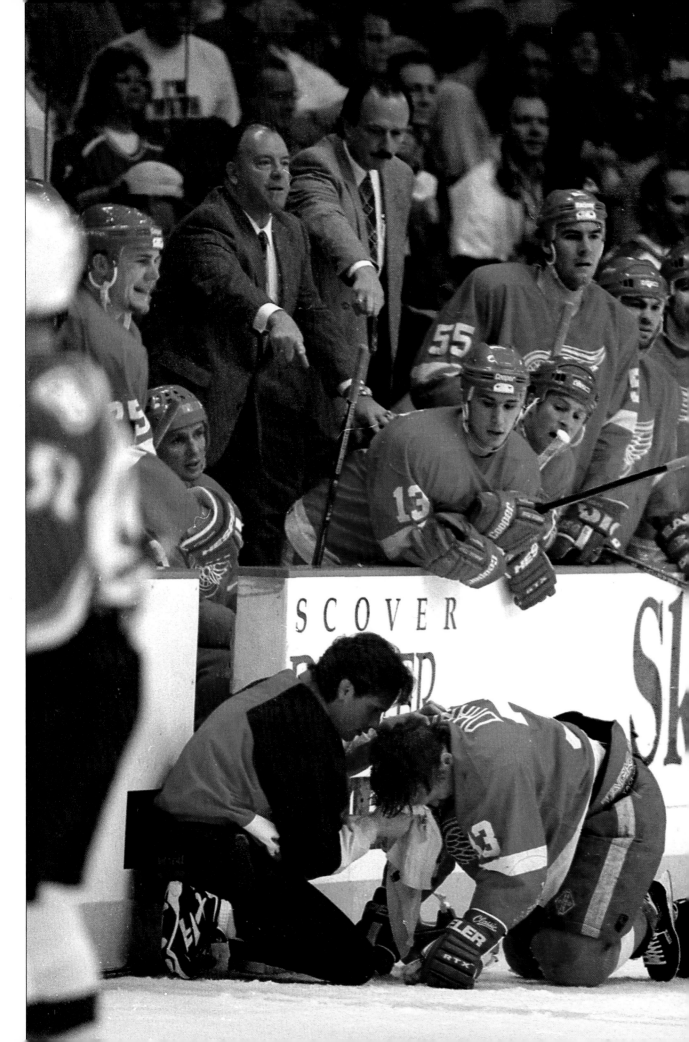

returned. The team might have been shuffled more drastically. And the most relevant lessons never would have been learned from the upcoming opponent, Colorado.

"Everyone dreams of shots like that," said Yzerman, who scored six goals in the series. "We talked about believing in our team. If anything, our will has gotten stronger, our confidence has grown."

From Bowman: "At some point, you have to have adversity."

The Wings had encountered some, apparently not enough. The grind was taking its toll and key players — Primeau, Paul Coffey — were battling injuries. The Avalanche showed up fearing nothing, and who knew it was a look we'd see in the Wings a year later.

Colorado attacked with hunger and size, with the irrepressible Patrick Roy and Claude Lemieux. Their stars — Joe Sakic, Peter Forsberg — played the best hockey of their lives, and in a brutal six-game battle, the Wings lost many of the scrums.

Lemieux caused emotional and physical damage, sucker-punching Vyacheslav Kozlov in one game, then the infamous hit, perhaps the most compelling thing to happen to the Wings in years. He crunched Kris Draper from behind, into the boards, and Draper's bloodied, crushed face was the symbol of the series. It was a wound that became a scar that became a badge that became a promise.

"We'll see him next year, and we're going to make it no secret what we're going to do to him,"

Osgood said. "It's stupid what he did, and it's the last time he's going to get away with it."

The Wings' anger would grow as Lemieux taunted them with jabs such as, "If they're concerned about retaliation for next year, that's a sad way to end a season."

For the Wings, it was the saddest way, their record accomplishments now mocking them. It also was the most important way, for now it was perfectly clear. They'd been fooled by success, lulled into trying again with a smallish team, but with this defeat, they learned more than they ever had, and dug the deepest well of motivation.

"We said all year the only thing that matters is working to be successful in the playoffs, and maybe we lost track of that," Yzerman said. "It's like we should take the regular season off and show up in April. This team wasn't good enough to win the Stanley Cup. Obviously, something has to be done different. We're close, but we're not there. Something has to change."

Finally, the acknowledgement. After the seven-game loss to San Jose, the Wings thought maybe it was a fluke. After the sweep by New Jersey, they figured their trip to the Finals had shaken them, and major changes weren't necessary. But another regular-season masterpiece followed by a playoff flop had convinced them it was time for the third step — Final Refining.

This is the tough one. Many teams reach the level of perennial contenders, few go farther. One

wrong move, one trade that's too risky, or not risky enough, can be the difference.

If the New Jersey series was the primer, Colorado hammered it home. Bowman had gotten caught up in all the sideshows, yelling at Lemieux in a parking lot, griping about the officiating. He was obsessed with how a game was called because he knew the Wings had to draw penalties to score goals.

After Game 6 in Denver ended, the Wings headed home, battered, bloodied ... enlightened. From that moment, everything that happened — brawls, suspensions, trades, words — built to the rematch in 1997, when the Wings could prove how studious they'd been.

In the off-season, Bowman traded Dino Ciccarelli, partly because he was small and getting old, partly because he took bad penalties against the Avalanche. Then, early in the season, Bowman sealed the deal that made it clear the Wings were attacking from a different angle. He traded Primeau and Coffey, playoff underachievers, to Hartford for Brendan Shanahan, acquiring size and spirit.

Later, he added Joe Kocur. He put together the Grind Line of Maltby, Kocur and Draper, and by the end of the season, it was getting as much playing time as the Russian unit. He gave tough rookie defenseman Aaron Ward more ice time.

Most important, Bowman and the Wings finally practiced what they had beseeched — that the regular season means nothing. They coasted to a 38-26-18 record, third in the

---

Center Kris Draper (33) was pummeled by Colorado's Claude Lemieux in Game 6 of the 1996 Western Conference Finals.

Western Conference. They held back so they could hold up when the games mattered. They watched the attention turn to Colorado, Dallas and Philadelphia, and privately, they relished their new role.

Oh, they had their 1996-97 regular-season moments. There was Bowman's 1,000th victory against Pittsburgh on Feb. 8, when Shanahan asserted himself with a hat trick. There was a 4-1 victory at Philadelphia, the first clue that the Wings could turn it on, when necessary.

The second clue came on March 26, the signature date, when Lemieux and the Avalanche came to town expecting to find the same broken Wings, and discovered things were different. Everything changed that night, the psychology of the rivalry, the dynamics of the season, the psyche of the Wings.

McCarty threw a punch he had spent a year coiling, and when Lemieux hit the ice and assumed the position, the Wings became the dominant team. The only thing left to do was prove it. Vernon fought Roy that game, Shanahan protected McCarty with a flying leap on Roy and the Wings won on an overtime goal by McCarty. The impact of that game cannot be minimized. The demons had been shooed, and free of the psychological baggage, the Wings were able to move forward.

"Maybe this is what we needed," Vernon said. "It shows we're willing to go to war for each other. This was the game that brought the Red Wings together. The boys were willing to pay the price."

By the time the playoffs hit, the Wings were hungrier, healthier, more physical, armed with precious knowledge, the only gift Colorado ever gave them.

They had the intangibles, the extra stride, the deepest well of emotion — revenge. They struggled early against St. Louis, and when the series was tied 2-2, Yzerman stood up in the dressing room and demanded more, starting with himself. It was a tangible sign he was leading, more than ever.

And now, it was the captain, the coach and the goalie. Vernon, given the full-time job because Bowman liked his experience and composure, was magnificent. Fighting for another year on his contract, he helped the Wings sweep Anaheim, winning three games in overtime.

Then came Colorado, which really was the final test, although Philadelphia awaited.

"If you're writing a script on how to get better, you take your last experience and figure out why you didn't advance," McCarty said. "We knew we had to get bigger. We knew we had to play disciplined. It's our job to dethrone them, and we believe we can do it."

They did it with such ferocity, they drove Avalanche coach Marc Crawford up a wall, or at least up a glass partition during Game 5, a 6-0 Detroit victory that featured a third period loaded with brawls. Crawford tried to get at Bowman, who watched with a bemused look, cool and confident, just like his team.

So many people answered so many

questions during that series, from Sergei Fedorov and his swift-skating Russian linemates, to Vernon, to grinders such as Martin Lapointe, McCarty and Maltby. The Wings had learned they were too small and too soft, and had brought in nastier players such as Shanahan, Tomas Sandstrom, Larry Murphy, Kocur and Ward to remedy it.

Once they dispatched the Avalanche, there was nothing to stop them. The Flyers became the Wings of 1995, and maybe the cycle begins for them. The cycle ended for the Wings two years after it began in a dank dressing room in New Jersey, where they gathered the information a championship team must collect.

The Wings' sweep of Philadelphia was brutally efficient, and again, they received help from all quarters, all lines. Vernon won the Conn Smythe, but the only trophy that mattered was the big silver one, hoisted by the captain, helped by the goalie, guided by the coach, surrounded by a true team.

"The great thing about this team was, everybody accepted their roles," Yzerman said. "We got goals and contributions from everyone. Everyone did their jobs, no questions asked."

No reason to ask. Questions had been posed for two years, across three seasons. History teaches, failure teaches. Champions learn. The Red Wings took a series of events and experiences and made a map out of them. They followed it from the lowest point to the highest point, where finally, finally, the cheers were all for them.

Vladimir Konstantinov (16) battles with the Flyers' Eric Lindros in 1996.

1996-97
Team of Destiny

A season full of magical moments

By Cynthia Lambert

The Detroit News

Destiny.

It's a quirky word believed by some, scoffed at by others. But if any one word could be used to describe the sentiment of the Red Wings in their first Cup-winning season in 42 years, that would be it.

"We are a team of destiny," Sergei Fedorov said throughout the playoffs.

Yet, when the Red Wings look back on this 1996-97 season, there will be ample material and events to sift through, presenting them with the reasons why it finally worked. As with any team that achieves great success, it is the sum of the parts, not one person or single event that is responsible for seeing the plan through.

But the success of the Wings did start with one obsessed man, who made trades, shifted lines and finally found the mix that worked. All he needed then was for the players to carry it out.

Scotty Bowman, in his fourth season as head coach of the Red Wings, started the 1996-97 season with a big trade to bring Brendan Shanahan to Detroit, a deal that will be viewed as the key.

Bowman had made other trades since taking over as director of player personnel in the summer of 1994.

His first deal was to trade defenseman Steve Chiasson to Calgary for Mike Vernon. The move was one of several key deals Bowman pulled off on the way to collecting the players he wanted for this Red Wings team.

But no trade was as crucial — or as difficult to pull off — than the one he made on Oct. 9 for Shanahan, a power forward the Wings knew they needed for two years. It was the one deal Bowman had to push for, the one he fought to consummate. And in the end, it might have been the deal that finally helped vault the Wings to their historic accomplishment.

"He's the total package," Bowman said of Shanahan, who scored 47 goals in the 1996-97 season.

But to get Shanahan, Bowman first had to convince team senior vice-president Jimmy Devellano that Shanahan was worth acquiring for disgruntled Keith Primeau, who had demanded a trade and was sitting at

home awaiting news, future Hall of Fame defenseman Paul Coffey and a No. 1 draft pick.

Wings captain Steve Yzerman helped the cause by telling Bowman that, from what he had observed during the World Cup of Hockey tournament, Shanahan was the real thing.

"Scotty fought for that trade, he fought it all the way," said Wings associate coach Barry Smith, a long-time friend of Bowman's.

The deal was one that went from on, to off, to back on again, all within a matter of days, and sometimes within hours. Bowman first thought he had the deal done on the morning of the team's season opener, Oct. 5, in New Jersey. He was so certain, he told Coffey to return home and went so far as to tell the defenseman he didn't care how he got there. The comment set off a string of controversy that Coffey refused to become part of, and bowed out of any com-

---

Overleaf: The Red Wings took flight after defeating Patrick Roy and the Avalanche on March 26, 1997.

Brendan Shanahan (14), Igor Larionov (8) and the Wings contained former teammate and Flyers defenseman Paul Coffey.

ments. And though the defenseman returned to practicing with the team over the next couple of days, he was told the afternoon of Oct. 9, the day of the Wings' home opener, that he was a member of the Hartford Whalers.

Earlier that day, Shanahan was told his dream job was a reality. He boarded a private jet sent by Wings owner Mike Ilitch and arrived at Joe Louis Arena minutes before the warm-ups started. In a show of unity and acceptance, Yzerman walked over to Shanahan, shook his hand and told him the team would not take the ice until he could go with them. Shanahan dressed hurriedly and skated out for what would be one of many key moments in the Red Wings' season of destiny. And after the game, his words supported the theory that he was just what Detroit needed.

"I am a piece but I don't see myself as a missing piece," Shanahan said. "This is a spectacular team. The important thing is to come to a town with the mandate to win the Stanley Cup. There is pressure from the city and the team puts pressure on itself.

"That's what I want. I like being in the big games, in the big moments. When I heard the fans cheering, I thought, this is the start of it, not the end of it. I welcome it."

The Wings fans welcomed Shanahan with hungry arms. Finally, that big, rugged winger was wearing the winged wheel.

The key dealings might have begun with Shanahan, but they didn't end there. Two other trades further helped Detroit's season come together. One was sending Greg Johnson to Pittsburgh for winger Tomas Sandstrom. The other was trading for Toronto defenseman Larry Murphy.

Not only did the two veteran players bring with them Cup-winning experience, but sizable contracts. Both factors showed again how badly the organization wanted to bring the Cup to Detroit.

"The fans and players, to some degree, felt we needed someone like Brendan, that type of player," defenseman Bob Rouse said. "But when they brought Murphy and Sandstrom here, that was another indication for us, the players. They were two veteran players making decent compensation. It showed the team was willing to do whatever it took to win. Both of those look like great moves now."

Not to be forgotten was Bowman's insistence on signing free agent and former Red Wings enforcer Joe Kocur. After losing Stu Grimson to the waiver wire in October, the team lacked a proven tough guy. And although he had played for the Red Wings Alumni team, a 30-and over beer league in the Detroit area, and finally with the San Antonio Dragons of the International Hockey League in December, Kocur looked as though he had never left the NHL. And ultimately, Kocur played regularly, even logging more ice time in the Finals, to help the checking line click.

All of those moves were made by one man — with the approval of many. They were made to bring the qualities Bowman felt necessary to win in the playoffs.

But Bowman also moved out those players he felt might hinder that process. His tenuous popularity took a serious hit before the season began, when he dispatched Dino Ciccarelli to Tampa Bay for a late-round draft

Russians Slava Fetisov and Vladimir Konstantinov (16), and Nicklas Lidstrom (5) helped anchor the Red Wings' defense.

pick, one of the most unpopular trades in recent memory.

"Say what you want about Dino, but the move gave more ice time to guys like Martin Lapointe and Darren McCarty," assistant general manager Ken Holland said. "It was a move that had to be made, to clear the way."

McCarty and Lapointe played key roles in the playoffs, unsettling opponents with their demeanor and startling them with their timely offense. Also leaving the team was forward Bob Errey, another player who was known to question Bowman's reasoning and demands.

What remained was a group determined to play without threat of mutiny. Even Yzerman, who had the credentials and the ability to challenge moves or strategy, kept his mouth shut and went along with Bowman's wishes.

"We're in no position to doubt what the winningest coach in the history of the game wants us to do," Kris Draper said. "I think this year we had to realize the accomplishments he's had. When you think about how he's won 1,000 games. I'm not talking about coaching 1,000 games, but actually winning 1,000. I look at how he's adapted over the years to the times and the players. It takes a lot to do that.

"We lost in the Cup Finals two years ago. But I look around the room in these Finals and everyone who was in this room was here because Scotty wanted them here. This is the team Scotty wanted and look what we were able to do."

But all of Bowman's moves were not for the better. By the end of the regular season, forward Sergei Fedorov — a former Hart Trophy winner as the league's MVP, and winner of the Selke Trophy as the league's best two-way forward — had

Darren McCarty (25) exacted revenge for his best friend and teammate, Kris Draper, by pummeling the Avalanche's Claude Lemieux.

played every position except goalie. His games on defense were the most challenging for a career forward who fought between keeping his feelings suppressed and venting to the media. The great experiment finally ended early in a first-round playoff series against St. Louis, when Bowman realized he needed to reunite the Russian Five. Once that move was made, Fedorov never returned to defense, and began to flourish up front.

Bowman tried a similar experiment with forward Mathieu Dandenault, playing him on defense and later playing with his mind. Dandenault, Detroit's second pick in the 1994 entry draft, was in the lineup for the first 48 games, but played in only 17 of the next 34. He didn't get

into a single playoff game and was left to wonder if he is a forward or defenseman. He was put in a position that seemed unnecessary and uncalled for.

Bowman also had to adjust to changes of his own. In December, Smith, his top assistant, was offered a head-coaching job in the Swedish Elite League. Smith took it, after being told by the team that if Bowman didn't return to coaching for the 1997-98 season he would not succeed him. Bowman encouraged Smith to take the job, but told him to return to Detroit in March after the Swedish league concluded. Then, before clearing it with upper management, Bowman hired former player Mike Krushelnyski as an assistant

and informed the media that Smith would return for the end of the regular season and the playoffs.

While Bowman worked for control of his staff, the Wings took control of their season in a game more remembered as an event, and one that will forever be remembered as the night the Wings didn't just get even, but pulled ahead.

Until the March 26 game against Colorado, the Wings not only had the playoff proving ground ahead of them, but putting some unfinished business from a May 29, 1996, playoff game in Denver behind them. That was the night the Wings were eliminated from the Western Conference finals, and also the night Claude Lemieux crushed Draper face-first into the boards. Draper sustained multiple facial fractures, displaced teeth and was put through further torture when he was faced with the fact that Lemieux and his Avalanche went on to sweep the Florida Panthers to win the Stanley Cup.

All of it was made worse because of Lemieux's refusal to apologize to Draper, and made unbearable with the Colorado forward's despicable comments regarding Draper's limited talents and how his hit made him a household word.

Every time Lemieux spoke, more fuel was poured on the Detroit fire. Even Shanahan, new to the scene and a friend of Lemieux's, took up the Red Wings' collective cause. Before the March 26 meeting, the first time Lemieux played in Detroit since the incident, Shanahan spoke of how he reveled in the fact that Lemieux was off balance, not knowing if Shanahan was a friend or foe.

"I want him wondering when he gets out there," Shanahan said the morning of the game. "He doesn't know how I feel about him and he won't know until game time."

Shanahan was the first to hit Lemieux in the game, and followed through by dumping him to the ice with a modified cross check. But the real fireworks exploded at 18:22 of the first period, when a seemingly insignificant hit by center Peter Forsberg on Igor Larionov set off a string of events that resulted in Lemieux's pummeling at the hands of McCarty at center ice.

"I don't know how we ended up together," McCarty would say with a smile after the game. "Maybe it was God's will."

Whatever the reason, McCarty took advantage of the situation and thoroughly spent himself on the player who rearranged his best friend's face.

"He looked right at me," McCarty said of Lemieux. "He didn't want any part of me, but he saw me coming. I wanted to make sure of that because I didn't want people thinking I wasn't fair about it."

As McCarty landed punch after punch to Lemieux, Avalanche goaltender Patrick Roy sprinted from his net to come to his teammate's aid. Before Roy could reach the main event, Shanahan charged onto the scene, intercepting Roy with a flying leap.

"We had a little bit of the WWF going there," Shanahan said later.

And as Adam Foote came to Roy's aid, Vernon came out of the Detroit net to even the match-up. The result was a slug-for-slug fight at center ice between Vernon and Roy — an almost humorous match-up with the 5-foot-9, 166-pound Detroit goalie squaring off against Roy, who is 6-0, 192.

"I did what anyone else in my position would have done," Vernon said.

Following the game — a 6-5 Detroit victory — Avalanche center Mike Keane labeled the Wings as gutless and heartless for not confronting Lemieux when the teams played 10

In an undercard to the March 26 slugfest, Wings' Mike Vernon squared off against Patrick Roy, leaving the Avalanche goalie worse for wear.

days earlier in Denver. They were comments that would continue to fuel the Wings throughout the season. And later, when the teams met in the Western Conference finals, they would haunt Keane.

But more significantly, that March 26 game gave the Wings a sense of closure for the previous season and opened up a new set of possibilities for what might lie ahead in the upcoming months. As ruthless and bloody as the night became, it showed to each Detroit player and to other clubs observing, that the Wings were a team, in every sense of the word.

"A game like this can help the confidence of the team and bring the guys together even more," Vernon said. "It was a good game all around. We made a lot of things happen. I don't think there's any question that it is the game that brought this team together."

That sense of unity was tested early in the playoffs, as the Wings struggled to manufacture offense and maintain momentum against the St. Louis Blues. The series started with Grant Fuhr stifling the Wings at Joe Louis Arena, 2-0. Detroit came back to win the next two games, but lost Game 4, 4-0, in St. Louis. The series was tied at two games apiece, and Game 5 was at Joe Louis Arena.

"Game 5 of the St. Louis series was when we showed we have a real team in this dressing room," defenseman Slava Fetisov said. "In that game we didn't depend on one or two guys. All four lines worked hard and contributed.

Detroit won Game 5, 5-2, a contest highlighted by the reuniting of the Russian Five. The Wings won Game 6, and the series, 3-1, on goals by Vyacheslav Kozlov, Shanahan and Kirk Maltby.

It would be the closest the Wings would feel to being eliminated in the playoffs. Their next round, against the Mighty Ducks of Anaheim, would be a sweep.

Three of the four games went into overtime, including triple overtime in Game 2. The clincher went 17:03 into the second overtime before Shanahan scored the winner. And as many of the players believed, Detroit's season of destiny showed itself through an interesting statistic that would ultimately test the Wings' patience.

"We kept saying that we played more overtime games than any other team," Shanahan said. "I think that was good preparation for this."

If the Wings learned discipline in the series against the Blues and patience against the Ducks, their overall mettle was pushed to its extreme in the rematch with the Avalanche in the Western Conference final.

Vernon, who had been strong in net until this point, was considered the weak link for Detroit compared to Roy's dominance in the playoffs for the Avalanche. Goaltending would be the key, it was predicted. How true. But it was Vernon who outshone Roy to put the Wings in the Cup Finals for the second time in three seasons after winning the series, 4-2.

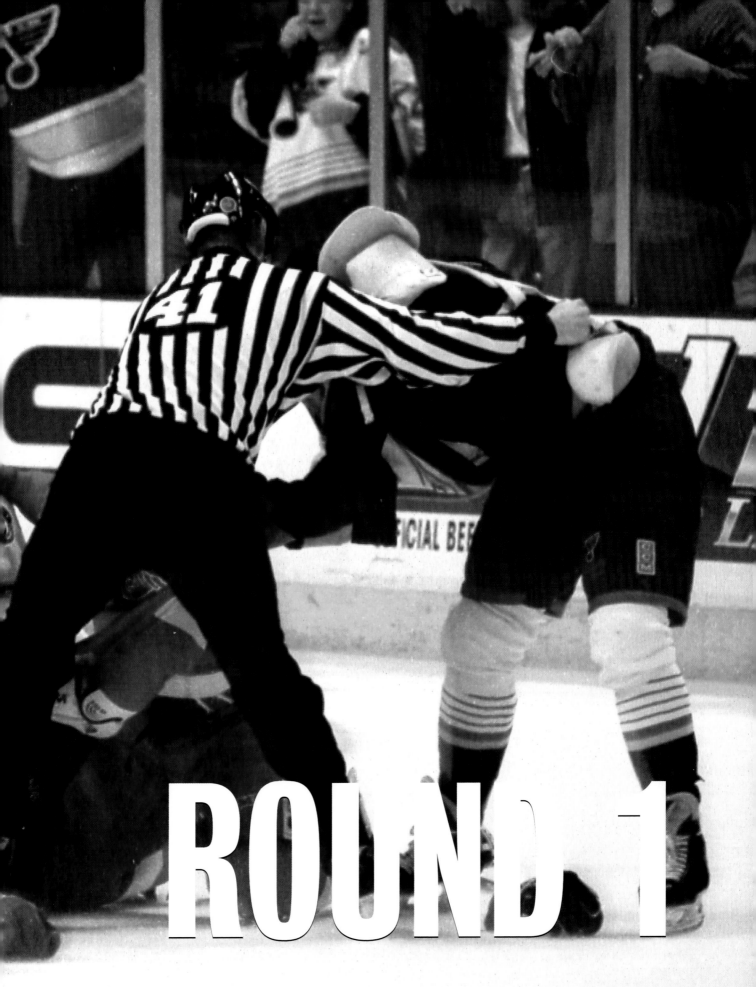

ROUND 1

BLUES FLATTEN WINGS IN OPENER

By Cynthia Lambert

The Detroit News

THE RED WINGS WERE ADAMANT THAT THE energy and enthusiasm were there. The problem was that those components were misdirected and misused.

What resulted was a 2-0 loss to the St. Louis Blues in Game 1 of the Western Conference semifinal. Game 2 is Friday at Joe Louis Arena.

"If anything, I think we were over-enthusiastic and a little uptight," Wings captain Steve Yzerman said.

Wings Coach Scotty Bowman agreed that the emotion the Wings lacked for the last two weeks of the regular season was back in full force. But instead of being an asset, it turned into a detriment, and the Wings took bad penalties.

"We have to harness our emotions a little better," Bowman said. "We had a lot of energy. But we were frustrated and took retaliation penalties. In a situation like this, you have to turn the other cheek. I know it's hard to do at a time like this, but you have to."

The Wings' plight was made worse early, when the Blues took a 2-0 lead in the first period. Geoff Courtnall scored the first goal at 12:54, when he popped a shot over a group of players near the crease, and goalie Mike Vernon was unable to stop it.

"We didn't cover it," Sergei Fedorov said. "The puck kept flying like a butterfly and into the net."

Pierre Turgeon scored on the power play at 19:22 of the first, when he redirected Al MacInnis' shot. The lead stood, thanks to the Wings' penchant for taking penalties and inability to score on the power play (0-for-7).

The poor performance negated excellent goaltending by Vernon in the second period, when he made 15 saves, several of which came during a five-on-three advantage for the Blues.

"It's tough to be down by two going into the second," Vernon said. "I think both teams came out kind of flat in

the first period. But all of a sudden, they were up by two goals."

The Wings managed 30 shots on Blues goalie Grant Fuhr, who was good when he needed to be, but wasn't overly taxed by the Wings.

"We have to find a way to beat Fuhr," Brendan Shanahan said. "We have to throw more at him and continue to get in his way."

If they don't do that, Fuhr could get in the way of the Wings' playoff run. "It's just one playoff game, though," Fuhr said. "We've got a lot of work to do still."

GAME 1

Red Wings

0

Blues

2

at Detroit
April 16, 1997

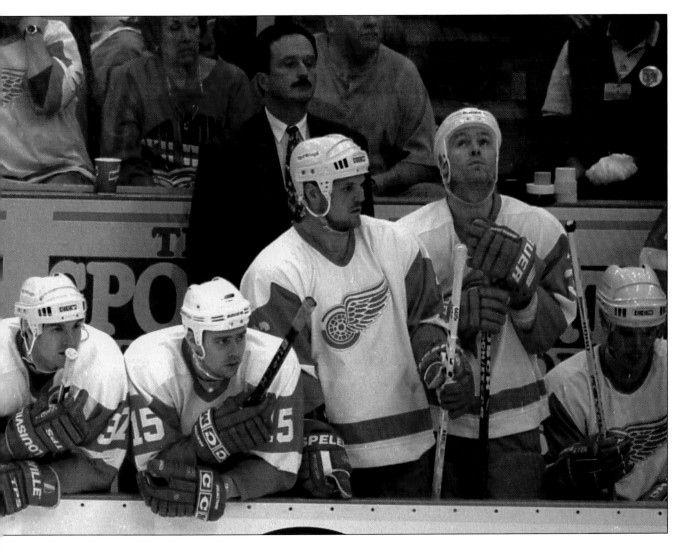

Goalie Mike Vernon (left) and the Red Wings started the post-season with a home loss to the St. Louis Blues.

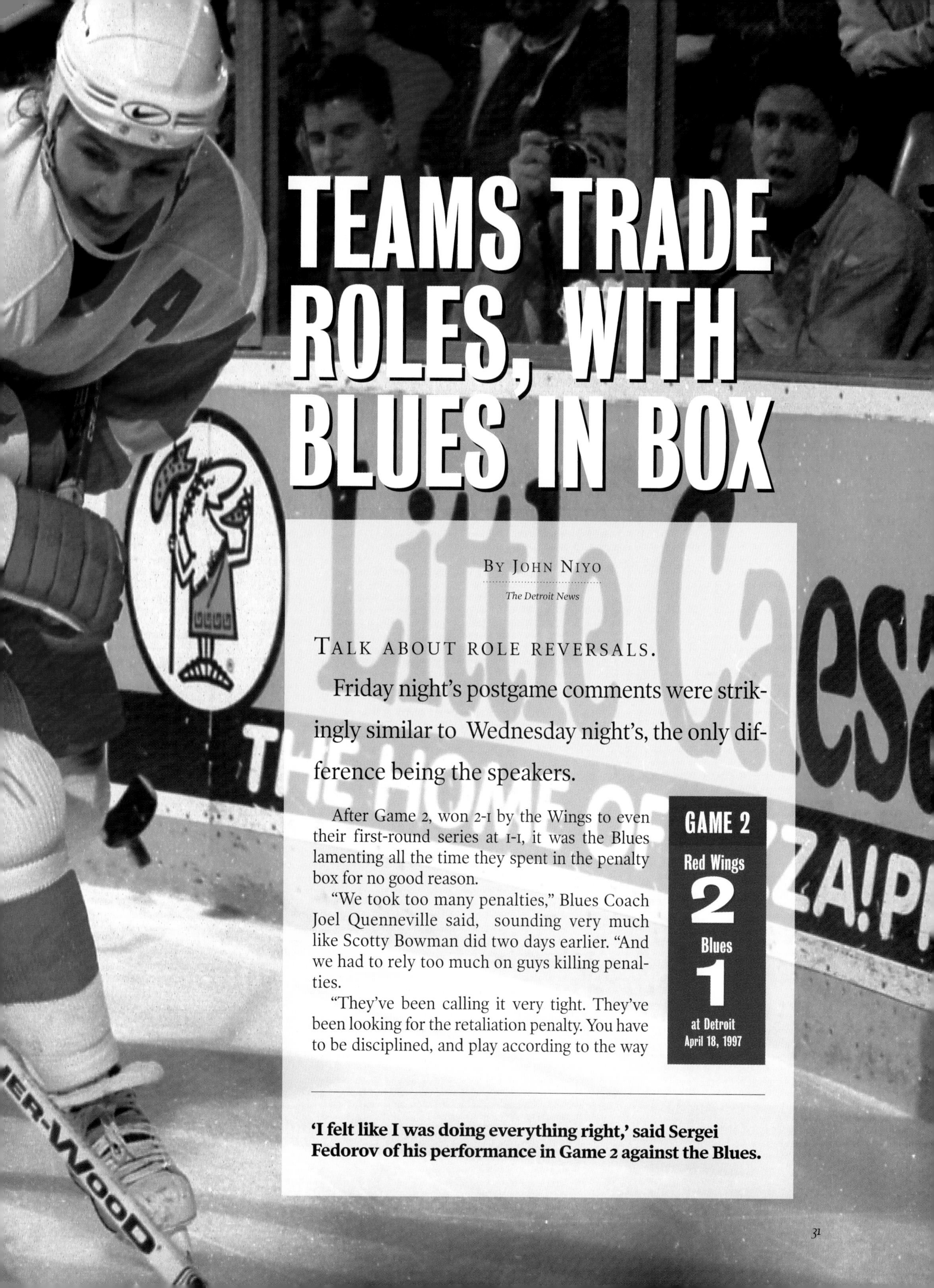

TEAMS TRADE ROLES, WITH BLUES' IN BOX

By John Niyo

The Detroit News

Talk about role reversals.

Friday night's postgame comments were strikingly similar to Wednesday night's, the only difference being the speakers.

After Game 2, won 2-1 by the Wings to even their first-round series at 1-1, it was the Blues lamenting all the time they spent in the penalty box for no good reason.

"We took too many penalties," Blues Coach Joel Quenneville said, sounding very much like Scotty Bowman did two days earlier. "And we had to rely too much on guys killing penalties.

"They've been calling it very tight. They've been looking for the retaliation penalty. You have to be disciplined, and play according to the way

GAME 2
Red Wings
2
Blues
1
at Detroit
April 18, 1997

'I felt like I was doing everything right,' said Sergei Fedorov of his performance in Game 2 against the Blues.

the refs call the game."

In Game 1, a 2-0 Blues' victory, the teams combined for 17 power-play opportunities — 10 for the Blues. In Game 2, there were 15 man-advantage situations.

Rarely were there 10 skaters on the ice Friday night at Joe Louis Arena, except, of course, for the two occasions where there were 11 — twice the Wings were penalized for too many men.

"There were just so many penalties," the Blues' Brett Hull said Friday night, sporting a fat lip courtesy of a Sergei Fedorov high stick.

"You can't rotate lines. It's makeshift lines ... kill a penalty, power play, kill a penalty, power play. There's no rhythm to the game, there was no 5-on-5, we kind of lost momentum. It was all special teams."

And for that, the Blues have only themselves to blame. It's not so much the referees have called the games tight, he said, but rather it's misdirected aggression.

"It's all the stupid penalties guys have been taking," said Hull, shaking his head. "That's the way the game's supposed to be called. You do something stupid, you deserve to go to the box. They got burned in Game 1, and we got burned tonight.

"The stupid part is we talked about it before the game. We said we've got to play the same way we did in Game 1. With our aggressive tenacity and hard work, force them to do the same thing they did the other night. We worked just as hard, but we were retaliating and taking bad penalties. That just kind of threw everything out of kilter."

Wings goalie Mike Vernon clears the puck before Blues forward Pierre Turgeon can take advantage of an open net in Game 2.

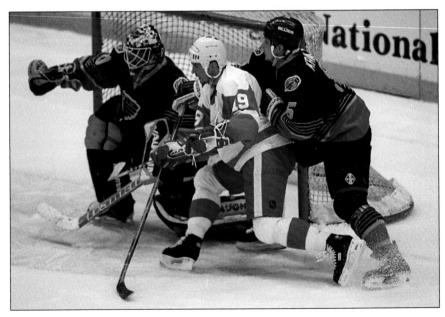

Blues defenseman Igor Kravchuk (5) tries to move the Wings' Steve Yzerman out of the crease and away from goalie Grant Fuhr.

Fedorov takes center stage

BY BOB WOJNOWSKI

The Detroit News

The smile is back. The acceleration and enthusiasm are back. Sergei Fedorov is back at center, where he belongs, the Wings are back in their playoff series. And one thing is readily apparent — to escape the muck that is St. Louis' defense, the Wings must ride and glide with their enigmatic star.

Brendan Shanahan is being targeted and neutralized. Steve Yzerman and Igor Larionov don't have the speed and strength to skate around stand-up defensemen. The Wings got goals from unheralded Kris Draper and Larry Murphy to win Game 2, 2-1, but it was Fedorov who changed the pace, who attacked so ferociously, the Blues' thin defense wore down.

This is Fedorov's series to control, as long as Scotty Bowman lets him. He can — and should — be the best player on the ice. Of course, that's been said for a while, then you watch his powerful rushes and remember why.

Someone has to be the star, and after years of deferring, after being maligned for sporadic effort, Fedorov must be the guy. Bowman's mad-scientist 10-game experiment with Fedorov on defense has to be over (please?) after Fedorov generated five prime scoring chances Friday night.

"I felt I was doing everything right," Fedorov said after playing 25 minutes at center. "I feel like I'm back. I just need that final touch. When you're bouncing around like a ball,

you never know what to expect. I was just a little bit rusty, I think."

Mike Vernon and Grant Fuhr have been spectacular in goal, canceling each other out. So this series is about finding pockets of opportunity on clogged ice. Only one player is capable of skating through the quagmire, and now that he's comfortable and confident, Fedorov just might do it.

Fuhr stopped him three times from point-blank range, and eventually, Fedorov will have to finalize. But for now, we'll settle for initiating, something he doesn't do often enough, or isn't allowed to do. He scored twice in 19 playoff games last year, a performance that cannot be repeated, not if the Wings are to advance.

"Obviously, I'm not Joe Sakic or Peter Forsberg, who get that opportunity," Fedorov said as the Wings prepared for Game 3 today.

"When I'm on the ice, I guess I'm the X guy. Whatever the team needs."

Can you be the difference in this series?

"Yes, I think so."

Fedorov feels it, his teammates feel it, and after challenging him all season, Bowman feels it, although he's still evasive about his plans. Sure, Fedorov can be moody and erratic. But to his credit, he did not lash out as he was shuttled from a checking line to defense.

Fedorov demands special attention on the ice, and frankly, special treatment off the ice. Bowman should

stop trying to make him into another good soldier and let him be a creative force. You don't make Van Gogh whitewash a fence and you don't play Fedorov on defense.

"He's one of the most explosive skaters I've ever seen," Shanahan said. "He can break through at any time. I know he's excited about being back at center."

The Blues do not share that excitement.

"He's more dangerous at center," Fuhr said. "He creates more chances, he gets more chances."

Fedorov was on the power play. He was on the penalty kill. He forced St. Louis' Pierre Turgeon to spend more time shadowing him and less time attacking.

Fedorov has a dramatic range of emotions. When he's down, he's way down. When he's up, he's exuberant. For now, he's exuberant.

"He had his jump back, they couldn't hold him down," Wings assistant coach Barry Smith said. "Everybody wants to feel important, and Sergei feels important again."

Rookies Aaron Ward and Jamie Pushor played well in their postseason debuts, freeing Fedorov to play center. Fedorov's contract is up, further incentive to skate hard. These Wings need every weapon and every star to fight off St. Louis. They need Fedorov, now more than ever. The encouraging thing is, they seem to know it, and so does he.

WINGS USE MAN-ADVANTAGE TO TAKE GAME-ADVANTAGE

BY CYNTHIA LAMBERT

The Detroit News

THE POWER PLAY ACCOUNTED FOR THE GOALS THE RED WINGS NEEDED to defeat the St. Louis Blues, 3-2, Sunday afternoon. But they weren't the reason the Wings won, giving them a two-games-to-one lead in a best-of-seven playoff series.

"Our composure is what won the game for us," Coach Scotty Bowman said.

The Wings reverted to the Biblical tactic of turning the other cheek.

Because of that, they spent 16:32 of the game with a man-advantage. For the afternoon, the Wings were 2-for-9 on the power play, breaking an 0-for-14 slump they brought into the game.

"And we should have scored more than that," said Steve Yzerman, who had one of the power-play goals, a redirection of Nick Lidstrom's slap shot from the left point.

The Wings' ability to resist retaliating after blatant penalties or

GAME 3

Red Wings

3

Flyers

2

at St. Louis
April 20, 1997

Grant Fuhr, who shut out the Red Wings in Game 1, allowed goals by Kris Draper, Brendan Shanahan and Steve Yzerman in Game 3.

Kris Draper gets together with former Red Wing Marc Bergevin during Game 3.

Steve Yzerman celebrates his winning goal in Game 3, giving the Wings a 2-1 series lead.

vicious hits stemmed from Bowman's words during Game 2, and a statement of fact from Bowman before Game 3.

"We had a bit of a meeting after the first period of Game 2," Joe Kocur said. "Scotty said it's up to the players, if we see a guy about to retaliate, to jump in. We're policing ourselves as much as anything."

In the first two games, the Blues had 18 power plays, a startling statistic Bowman used to help support his theory of self-discipline, voiced to the players before Sunday's game.

"I think the players realized the effect it can have," Bowman said. "We had 18 shorthanded situations for two games. I showed them that in the New Jersey and Anaheim (series),

there were eight shorthanded situations. That's a big difference."

Kris Draper, as he did in Game 2, scored the Wings' first goal. This time it was the first of the game, 2:40 into the first period.

"The way the games have been going, it was perfect timing," Draper said. "Instead of waiting for the third period to get the lead. I guess the goal could have been a lift or a spark."

On a giveaway by Lidstrom, the Blues tied the score at 17:09 of the first when Brett Hull's slap shot beat Mike Vernon. But Brendan Shanahan and Yzerman sandwiched power-play goals around one by Joe Murphy in the second period to make it 3-2.

Killing power plays for almost half the game undercuts St. Louis

By John Niyo

The Detroit News

INITIATE, DON'T RETALIATE. THAT WAS JOEL QUENNEVILLE'S MESSAGE TO his St. Louis Blues before, during and after Sunday afternoon's game at the Kiel Center.

He can only hope that — eventually — his players will listen.

Choosing his words carefully, Quenneville said after a frustrating 3-2 loss: "I think as the series progresses you'll see a lot more five-on-five hockey."

A quick scan of the score sheet told the story Sunday. The Blues'

penalties in Game 3 were for cross-checking, roughing, slashing, roughing, high-sticking, high-sticking (again), head-butting, cross-checking ... and another slashing for good measure.

"I think the word for tonight's game is 'undisciplined,'" the Blues' Al MacInnis said, with more than a

hint of sarcasm. "It never fails, the referees aren't quick enough to catch the initiation. It's the retaliation penalties they catch. We just can't play that way and expect to win against a team like Detroit. ... We need controlled emotion out there."

With an emphasis on controlled.

Sunday, they got little of that. And

Mike Vernon and the Red Wings tripped up the Blues at the Kiel Center, reclaiming the home-ice advantage.

the penalties were hard to argue with.

"They could have been shorthanded the whole game," Wings Coach Scotty Bowman said, chuckling.

"We played right into their hands," admitted Marc Bergevin, who was among the few innocent Blues despite playing nearly half of Sunday's game.

The Blues were whistled for 10 penalties — 33 minutes' worth, to be exact — and spent a large portion of the afternoon shorthanded.

"You're not gonna win when you're killing penalties 33 minutes out of 60," said Brett Hull, who also lament-

ed the lack of discipline after Game 2 Friday night. "That's the game as far as I'm concerned."

Particularly damaging were penalties taken by 16-year veteran Craig MacTavish, for high-sticking Kirk Maltby in the final minute of the first period, and rookie Jim Campbell, for cross-checking Bob Rouse in the third period. The Wings scored on both ensuing power plays, and that proved to be the difference.

But the guilty parties were numerous Sunday. (Take a bow, Geoff Courtnall and Joe Murphy.)

Courtnall's bonehead play — head-

butting Maltby — didn't result directly in a goal, but it did mean five minutes more of killing penalties for a team already playing with a shortened bench. Murphy took a double-minor for a flagrant high stick that cut Kris Draper.

"It's up to the individuals to control their emotions. A lot of the game is played from the shoulders up, you know?" said MacInnis, another 16-year veteran, who serves as a tri-captain and is not easily riled up.

The Blues' star player agreed.

"You've got to be smart," Hull said, shaking his head. "

BLUES GET EVEN AT KIEL

Fuhr Blanks Wings, Courtnall Scores Twice

BY CYNTHIA LAMBERT
The Detroit News

THERE WERE NO KRIS Draper heroics on Tuesday night for the Red Wings. There were no Detroit heroics, period, and the St. Louis Blues defeated Detroit 4-0 to even the best-of-seven series at two games apiece.

Game 5 will be played Friday at Joe Louis Arena, giving the teams two days to rest and reflect.

Geoff Courtnall (two), Pavol Demitra and Chris Pronger scored for the Blues, and goalie Grant Fuhr made 28 saves en route to his second shutout of the series.

The Blues took a 2-0 lead into the third period, along with most of a power play left over from the second.

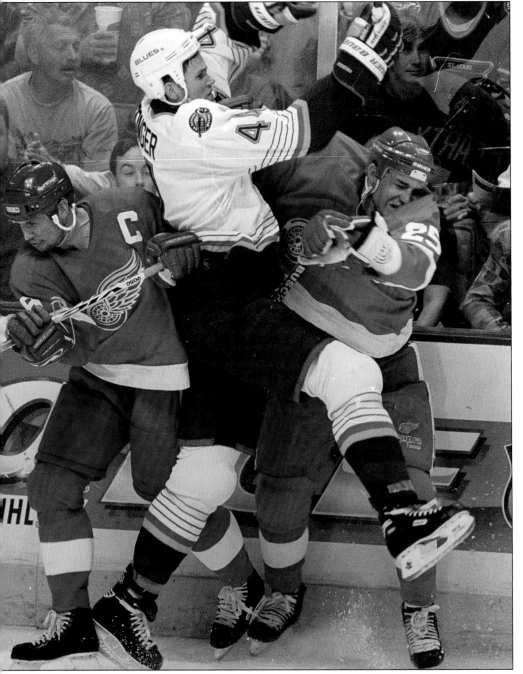

Steve Yzerman and Darren McCarty, right, sandwich Chris Pronger.

And at 1:10, Courtnall took a pass from Demitra and beat goalie Mike Vernon to increase the St. Louis lead to 3-0.

Shortly after the goal, Vladimir Konstantinov took an elbowing penalty. Upon sitting in the penalty box, he tried a number of times to cover the lens of the box video camera by using his stick to lift a towel.

When that didn't work, he used his hands to block any visual of him serving the penalty. All of this was seen on the arena big screen and drew delighted chants of "U.S.A." from the crowd of 19,787 at the Kiel Center.

The crowd was pleased further when Pronger scored on a breakaway

GAME 4

Red Wings

0

Blues

4

at St. Louis
April 22, 1997

at 9:23 , sent in by Demitra. After that goal, Coach Scotty Bowman replaced Vernon with Chris Osgood, who made his first appearance of the playoffs.

Vernon faced 23 shots, and Osgood faced his first seconds after he got into the net, when he turned aside a Pronger shot.

The third period also featured more penalties than had been called

in the previous two. Referee Mark Faucette called a more forgiving style of game, in part, resulting in only three minor penalties through the first two periods. But as the score got more lopsided, the chippy play also increased, culminating in a full-ice brawl that included both goaltenders, with 1:21 left to play. At the same time, some fans tried to get involved, pelting the Detroit bench with debris. A total of 118 penalty minutes was called for the melee.

The four-goal margin tied for the Wings' worse loss of the season.

They lost 6-2 at Toronto on Nov. 2.

Things got a little 'chippy' in the third period after the Blues took a big lead in Game 4.

RED WINGS' HOTTEST LINE CONTINUES TO GRIND

BY JOHN NIYO

The Detroit News

THE T-SHIRT WAS BARELY A DAY OLD, AND ALREADY IT'S A COLLECTOR'S item. Kirk Maltby, nattily dressed in a suit and tie after the Wings' 5-2 victory Friday night in Game 5 of the first round series with St. Louis, tried to hide it behind his back as he exited the Wings' dressing room. But Darren McCarty wouldn't let him: "Show it to 'em," he goaded.

And so, sheepishly, Maltby unveiled the new shirt, which features caricatures of himself, Kris Draper and Joey Kocur proudly under the slogan "The Grind Line."

That forward unit had been the only consistent one for the Wings through the first four games of this playoff series with St. Louis. On Friday night, there was a slight change, but the results were the same.

McCarty filled in for Kocur at right wing, and the new-and-improved Grind Line — which scored to make it 3-1 — was a force again. Even Scotty

GAME 5

Red Wings

5

Blues

2

at Detroit
April 25, 1997

Bowman said so.

"I think the key to the game, really, was the play of Draper, McCarty and Maltby," an unusually effusive Bowman said after the game. "They played against all of the St. Louis lines.

They scored a big goal to really get us going — the kind of goal we need, going to the net, picking up the rebound. I thought they did a tremendous job.

"They played more than they have in a long time, Draper and Maltby especially"

McCarty had been getting plenty of ice time, skating first on the Wings' top line with Igor Larionov and Brendan Shanahan and, in Game 4, with Sergei Fedorov and Steve Yzerman.

"I've been kidding him about it," Draper said, laughing. "You know, 'Remember your roots.' Maybe this'll bring him back to reality. Any time you get a chance to play with one of

Darren McCarty, a member of the Grind Line, had a goal in Game 5 against the Blues.

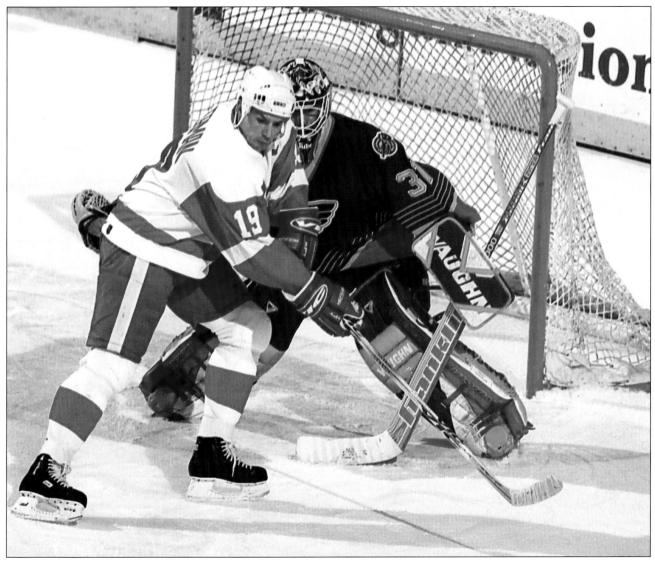

Steve Yzerman and the Wings moved closer to eliminating Grant Fuhr and the Blues after Game 5.

those guys — Stevie, Shanny, Sergei, Igor — and then you have to go with Drapes? I guess, it is a little bit of a demotion. But he handled the demotion well."

A demotion? Hardly. Said McCarty, laughing: "C'mon, it's the hottest line in hockey."

That might be a bit of an exaggeration, but the truth is, Draper & Co. are finding some scoring success after a disappointing regular season.

Draper has two goals in the first four games against the Blues. McCarty scored Friday night on a rebound after Larry Murphy's centering pass deflected off Draper's skate — just the way they diagrammed it.

"Murph was actually throwing me the one-timer, and Drapes wanted to get in on the play," McCarty said, tongue-in-cheek.

"I was just trying to get out of the way," Draper said. "I saw Murph coming in, so I just tried to pull out to cover him. And it hit my skate, went on goal, and Mac was there to bang the rebound in.

"Our line doesn't do anything fancy, but it's a fun line to play with. Each of us knows what the others are going to do. Nobody's gonna pull any punches. And it's not gonna be fancy hockey. We just kind of go out and crash and bang and go to the net."

Wings' wishes rest on stars

BY BOB WOJNOWSKI

The Detroit News

It's the simplest rule of success. You put your best people in the best positions. Your best salesman works your biggest buyer. Your best circus worker tames the lion. Your best baker does the wedding cakes.

Your best players control the biggest games. The Red Wings know this, and now, they're finally in a position to prove it. The Russian Five are skating together full-time again, building confidence. Steve Yzerman and Brendan Shanahan are playing together again, building confidence. With that familiar flair, the Wings were flying again in a 5-2 victory Friday night against St. Louis to take a three-games-to-two series lead.

Today, the Wings can clinch the series, or cinch their reputation as a team that vexes and perplexes. They have fiddled around long enough. Scotty Bowman has fiddled around long enough. The Wings' stars promised they'd do their jobs, and they did. Yzerman, Shanahan, Darren McCarty and Vyacheslav Kozlov (remember him?) scored, helping Detroit equal its four-game goal total in one night.

The Wings were still smiling Saturday, as if a weight had been lifted. The weight will return — extra big, extra heavy — if the Blues win today to force a Game 7, but for the first time in a tough series, the Wings feel like themselves again, and look like themselves again.

"I could feel it in the dressing

The Wings' stars — Steve Yzerman, top, and Brendan Shanahan, above — finally came through in the playoffs against the Blues.

room, on the bench and on the ice," said Slava Fetisov, elder skatesman on the Russian Unit. "Before this, it was just random hockey."

Bowman loves randomness, worships unpredictability. Sometimes it works. And sometimes, your best people must be in the best positions. For the first time in months, Shanahan played regularly on a line with Yzerman and Martin Lapointe, and it produced three goals. Through four games, Yzerman and Shanahan had combined for three points.

"You've got to be confident and loose to score goals," Shanahan said. "Everyone contributed, and that alleviates pressure on a few guys. ... The Russians change the outlook of the team because they're an element that's so difficult to check. They're so patient with the puck; if I was out there, I'd probably shoot and kill the play."

We knew Shanahan and Yzerman would rise, eventually. We had our doubts about the Russian unit, which had played well in brief spurts during the series and the season. Finesse skating and pretty passing generally get crushed in the playoffs, but as a change of pace, as a rabbit punch amid head blows, it showed wonderful potential.

Led by the dizzying creativity of Igor Larionov and the power skating of Sergei Fedorov, the unit befuddled St. Louis. It produced one goal, but it also worked as a defensive force, keeping possession from the Blues like kids playing keep-away.

"We understand each other better than anyone," Fetisov said. "It makes

it easy for us, not so easy for them. We control the puck 90 percent of the time. They can put their biggest guys against us and never touch the puck."

That healthy brashness might be returning. Some of the Russians admit they pass too much, but they consistently create scoring chances, even if they don't cash in. Fedorov and Kozlov, especially, seem energized when reunited.

"We can draw attention away from Steve and Brendan," said Fedorov, still seeking his first goal. "We surprised our opponent with all kinds of plays, all kinds of goals. We feel very good about it, very excited."

That's obvious to everyone, which means there's, oh, a 60-40 chance Bowman will keep the lines intact, including the new "grind line" of McCarty, Kris Draper and Kirk Maltby.

You can never get too comfortable, and if the Wings assume they'll unleash another barrage today, they haven't learned a thing. But you can't get too confused, either. Sometimes, familiarity breeds success.

"We can't think we have any breathing room," Shanahan said. "We played like we had something to prove — and we still haven't proven anything."

Well, they've proven a little. Now that they're in proper strike positions, they have a chance to prove more.

Mike Vernon was the saving grace in goal to help the Wings gain an advantage over the Blues in Game 5.

WINGS WASH AWAY THE BLUES

By Cynthia Lambert
The Detroit News

THE RED WINGS DIDN'T want to leave anything to chance. So they ended their first-round series at the first opportunity, winning 3-1 Sunday at the Kiel Center and eliminating the St. Louis Blues four games to two.

"You really don't know what will happen if it goes to a Game 7," Steve Yzerman said. "Last year, it took double overtime in Game 7 to win it. You don't want to put yourself in that position."

Instead, the Wings fed off the momentum from their Game 5 victory in Detroit. Then they stomped on the Blues' confidence early.

"We have to close down some teams," associate coach Barry Smith said. "We didn't want to give them that light, that added incentive. You don't want to give teams a break."

The Wings recovered quickly after falling behind in the opening minutes on a goal by Brett Hull.

Vyacheslav Kozlov scored on a

GAME 6

Red Wings
3

Blues
1

at St. Louis
April 27, 1997

power play 8:45 into the first to tie the score entering the second. Brendan Shanahan got his third goal of the series when he scored off a nice goal-mouth pass from Tomas Sandstrom 1:07 into the second. Kirk Maltby's goal 8:24 into the third sealed the victory. It was his first in 14 career playoff games.

"The third goal was a big goal," Coach Scotty Bowman said. "Maltby and (Kris) Draper were the difference for us."

The Draper-Maltby-Darren McCarty line — dubbed the Grind Line — accounted for four goals in the six-game series. Draper had two, and Maltby and Darren McCarty one each. Although the Russian Five and the Shanahan-Yzerman line drew much of the Blues' attention, the Draper line provided a spark when the Wings needed it most.

"Our line had lots of chances at the end of the season, but we couldn't score," Maltby said. "It's good to get some now. More than anything, we didn't want it to go another game. We didn't want a one-game win-or-lose situation. We battled back and played hard."

On five power plays, the Blues managed one routine shot.

"They did a great job of checking us," Coach Joel Quenneville said. "We didn't come up with many loose pucks, or any loose pucks."

The Wings can rest for a few days. They won't know their second-round opponent until the first round is completed Tuesday night.

Vyacheslav Kozlov is the first to congratulate Mike Vernon after the Wings bounced the Blues.

Patchwork turns into art work

BY BOB WOJNOWSKI

The Detroit News

Bit by bit, shot by shot, save by save, we began to see what we thought we'd see. We saw a veteran goaltender making big-moment saves. We saw a sniping star score big-moment goals. We saw the Russian unit control the puck and the Grind Line make the Blues eat the puck. We saw the Red Wings finish St. Louis as good playoff teams do, with authority.

This was the one the Wings had to win, Game 6, on the road, before Grant Fuhr began to believe everything being said about him. Their 3-1 stuffing of St. Louis was oh so important, not just because it was the clincher, not just because they get a few days rest, not just because they defused the pressure before it mounted.

This was telling because, for the second straight game, the Wings showed more of the pieces needed in the playoff puzzle. This team was rebuilt for this time of year, and three of its four victories were fraught with tension and loaded with grit.

Mike Vernon proved he can be the solid (and occasionally spectacular) goalie you need. Brendan Shanahan,

with the winning goal Sunday and three in the series, showed he could be the key-moment scorer. Kirk Maltby, who got his first playoff goal, showed he and Kris Draper can provide the third-line input you need.

Now, we're not suggesting the Wings are suddenly playoff heavyweights. We're just saying they handled the Blues more easily than last year (when St. Louis didn't have Fuhr) and learned a bit along the way.

"We didn't play over our heads, nothing extraordinary," captain Steve Yzerman said. "We never got derailed. Maybe it's just experience. We've seen a lot of situations."

In the playoffs, the less you rely on the extraordinary, the better your chances. Vernon didn't have to stop all the pucks. Shanahan and Yzerman didn't have to score all the goals. Heck, Sergei Fedorov didn't have to score any, although that must change.

This is not a one-guy, one-line, one-style team. With the Russian unit, the Wings can outskate anyone. Draper, Maltby and Darren McCarty can crash into nets, boards and bodies. The stars — Shanahan, Yzerman, Fedorov — must contribute the most, obviously, but at least the Wings know the other pieces work, none more important than Vernon.

"Mike gives us confidence," Scotty Bowman said. "When you play against guys like Fuhr and Patrick Roy, who have won so much, it's like going against a great pitcher. You need a good pitcher to match them."

When the Blues attacked early in the third period, Vernon didn't flinch. He made a big save on Geoff Courtnall and kicked everything wide, out of rebound danger.

Vernon has been a picture of poise, lending a calm to a team that has had a tendency to turn squirrelly at the first bad goal. He shrugs off praise and redirects questions about himself as adeptly as he kicks away pucks. This is a guy who knows how quickly it can turn, and this is a team that realizes the same.

In the last two games, including the 5-2 pasting of St. Louis on Friday night, the Wings played with composure we weren't positive they had.

"When they came at us in the third period, we didn't show any signs of panic," Shanahan said. "To be honest, we did a lot of the same things all series, it just started to work. No secret philosophies — just put the puck on the net and go after it."

It helps when St. Louis' Pierre Turgeon sticks his tippy-toes in the crease, wiping out a score-tying goal. The NHL does need to adjust its zero-tolerance policy for crease situations, but frankly, the Wings played well enough to earn breaks, and they got a few. Even the Blues noticed these Wings are constructed differently, talking afterward about their grittier style.

So the first series is done, the first returns are in, the first benefits of retooling have been recorded. There are signs this run will be different, if it's a run at all. The Wings must play better, of course, but they showed enough glimpses to make us suspect they can.

Brett Hull greets former teammate Brendan Shanahan after the Wings' series-clinching win.

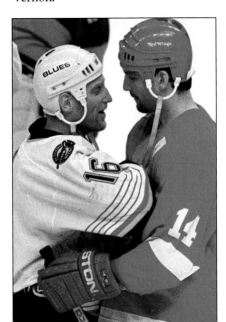

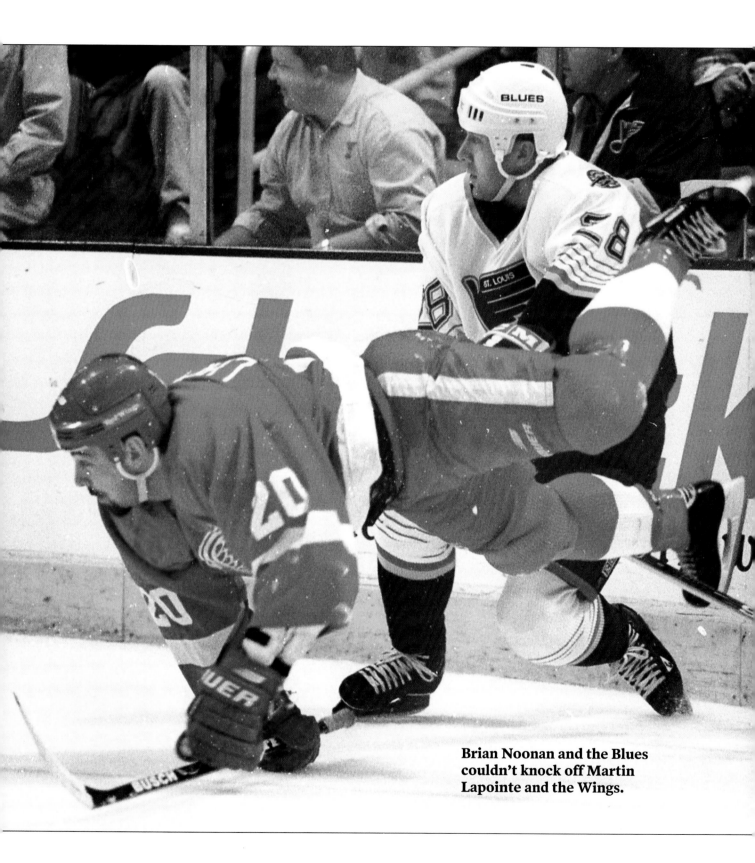

Brian Noonan and the Blues couldn't knock off Martin Lapointe and the Wings.

ROUND 2

LAPOINTE WORKS OVERTIME FOR GAME–WINNER

BY CYNTHIA LAMBERT AND JOHN NIYO

The Detroit News

GAME 1

Red Wings

2

Ducks

1

at Detroit
May 2, 1997

FORGET ABOUT THAT TEAM CONCEPT for a second. Just for a moment.

"You always want to be the hero," Martin Lapointe admits. And in hockey, heroes are made in the playoffs. Everybody knows that.

Friday night, Lapointe got his wish — much to the delight of his teammates and the 19,983 fans at Joe Louis Arena — scoring the overtime goal that gave the Wings a 2-1 victory and a 1-0 series lead over Anaheim.

Lapointe created the chance in the first minute of overtime by digging the puck out of a scrum near the boards and, while falling down, sending a pass to Brendan Shanahan, who was skating free toward center ice.

Then Lapointe quickly "got off his (butt)" — Darren McCarty's descrip-

tion — and joined the rush.

"Marty's a spirited player," Wings Coach Scotty Bowman said. "He made a good play back at the blue line. He worked hard with (Larry) Murphy and then he made the play to go to the net."

Said Lapointe: "I just saw the puck pop up, and I saw Shanny on my left side so I got it to him because he was ahead of me. I realized at that point it was a 2-on-1, so I just went to the net. He gave me a great pass and I one-timed it."

Of course, Lapointe was just as

surprised as everyone else when Shanahan decided to pass rather than shoot.

"Well, Shanny's a 50-goal scorer, and I'm a 16-goal scorer," Lapointe said, laughing. "But I thought to myself, 'I better get ready. It's a 2-on-1 and you can win the game.'"

He did. And, he did.

"I one-timed it, I didn't even look," said Lapointe, who, by his estimation,

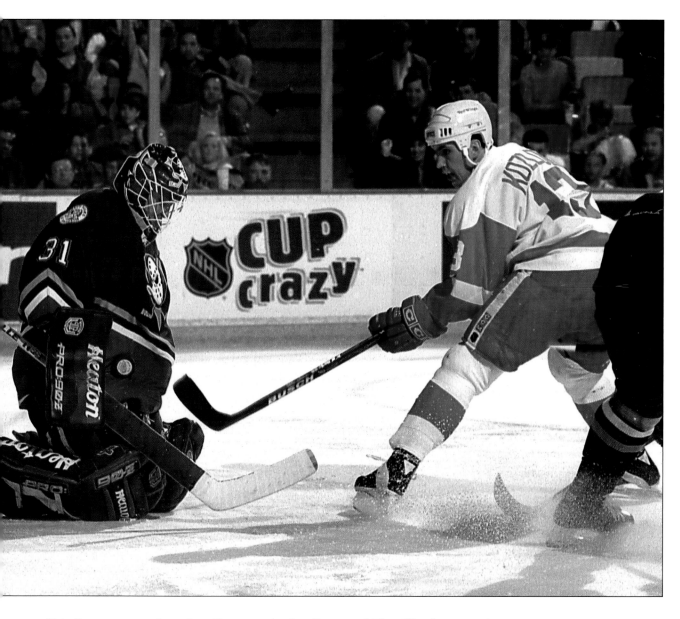

scored his first-ever overtime playoff goal on any level. He had but one other NHL playoff goal to his credit before Friday.

But without so much as a glance, he put the Wings on the right path to start this conference semifinal series. In round one against St. Louis, a Detroit loss in the opener virtually guaranteed an extended series.

The Wings are enjoying this new game they've discovered: Playoff hockey the way it was meant to be played.

"We're pretty confident," Lapointe said. "We just said, 'Keep shooting at him. And get in front of him.' Sergei's goal was like that.

"(Goalie Guy Hebert) didn't see the puck. We need more goals like that."

Shoot first, last and always. That's the Wings' mantra in these playoffs.

Mighty Ducks goalie Guy Hebert stopped Vyacheslav Kozlov and the Red Wings for most of Game 1 of the Western semifinals.

Everyone else is doing it, why not them?

"It doesn't matter where you are," Lapointe said. "I mean, look at (Anaheim's Paul) Kariya. Every time he has the puck just before the blue line he lets it go. That's the kind of shots we've got to take. He scores a lot of goals like that. We've got to do that."

As for Lapointe, the goal wasn't the only highlight of his night.

Bowman, looking for an offensive spark, shuffled his lines throughout Game I. And for a few shifts, Lapointe found himself on Kris Draper's famed checking line.

"I played with the Grind Line tonight," said Lapointe, smiling at the honor.

Then he was paired with Sergei Fedorov and Slava Kozlov. And finally, he was skating with Steve Yzerman and Shanahan, with whom he teamed up for the winner.

Mike Vernon, in net for the seventh straight playoff game, make 19 saves against the Ducks and shrugged off his performance in the opener.

"There's always pressure on the goaltender," Vernon said. "My job is to keep our team within striking distance."

But facing a team like the Mighty Ducks, who have a stingy defense, means Vernon can only give up one or two goals to keep his team in the game. He doesn't consider that any more daunting than going up against the Blues' Grant Fuhr, whom the Wings faced and defeated in the first round.

"We just faced a guy in St. Louis who shut us out twice," Vernon said. "It's tough when you're in a situation like that, but you have to keep bearing down. You have to keep competing and battling."

Ducks are boring, but can't lull Wings

By Bob Wojnowski

The Detroit News

Zzzzzzzzzz ... snork ... zzzz ... hmmphh ... cough, cough ... huh? What? Sleeping? Who was sleeping?

Not me. No sir. I was busy watching the Mighty Dull Ducks of Anaheim play the Red Wings in Game I of a Western Conference semifinal. I was thoroughly entertained for, goodness, 10, 11 seconds at a time. I was especially enthralled by that play in which four Ducks sit in a row in the neutral zone and sort of swat at the puck, and when one of them gets it, he makes a dazzling move, turns and dumps it down the ice.

This isn't Duck Soup. We would not be so cliche. This is Duck Muck — muck and chuck. If you watched the Wings grind through it for a 2-1 overtime victory Friday night, you know what I mean. This will be one boring series, absolutely soccer-like.

If the Wings advance — as I suspect they will, in five or six games — they can send game tapes to sleep clinics across the country.

Do not misunderstand. This is not intended to demean the Ducks, not any more than Disney already demeans them. They're tenacious and disciplined and they have two flashy stars, Paul Kariya and Teemu Selanne — two mallards surrounded by plucky ducklings.

They're frustrating to play and irritating to watch and in a strange way, their stifling style is the perfect test to see if the Wings have learned their lesson.

"For us, it's annoying; for them, it's very smart," Wings forward Darren McCarty said. "It's tough, but you can't let it bother you."

Oh, it has made the Wings twitch and sweat in the past. Didn't St. Louis take them to seven games in last year's playoffs merely by aggravating them? Didn't New Jersey pound them in the 1995 Stanley Cup Finals with a suffocating neutral-zone trap the Wings simply couldn't beat, and eventually stopped trying?

We've said it before: These Wings seem different, more disciplined, less prone to anxiety attacks. They eliminated the Blues this year with poise in the last two games and they showed it again Friday night, as Anaheim's Guy Hebert was shutting them out until Sergei Fedorov lifted the tension with the goal we've been waiting to see.

"The difference is, we don't have as many offensive players, so when we don't score, it's not as big a shock to us," captain Steve Yzerman said. "It's like when Mike Tyson gets hurt a little bit. He's not used to it, so all of a sudden, he falls apart. He can't adjust."

The Wings can adjust, and if they think their victory proves it,

Mighty Ducks goalie Guy Hebert has a stifling, disciplined defense in front of him.

they'd better prepare to prove it again. Because in the Ducks' dressing room, confidence is bubbling.

This, after all, is a team that finished nine points behind the Wings and was 3-0-1 against them while accidentally permitting three goals.

"We proved we could play with them," defenseman Bobby Dollas said after Game 1. "But give them credit. They played patient, too. They waited for us, we waited for them."

We waited for something compelling to happen. The Joe Louis Arena fans waited, periodically booing to let us know they were still there. The only difference between the game and the intermissions was, during intermissions, the Zamboni made more end-to-end rushes.

Obviously, the safe, defensive style employed by less-talented teams like Anaheim is bad for hockey, good for playoff success. Until Commissioner Gary Bettman fixes it and allows skating and creativity to become relevant elements again, the Ducks are smart to play it, and the Wings are smart to accept it.

"We'll play the exact same way (today)," Hebert said. "We'll clog up the neutral zone and try to get another 1-0 game. It puts more pressure on them."

And don't even attempt to mention the B-word to a Duck.

"Boring?" Coach Ron Wilson said. "Is winning boring? I'd rather win boring than lose exciting. ... This isn't the style I want to play; it's the style

we have to play."

It is a sound principle, I suppose. Don't take chances. Don't aggressively fore-check and risk getting caught up ice. Wait for the other team to goof, then burn them. It's hockey today, where nullifying talent is more important than showcasing talent.

The Wings have come to understand it, largely because Scotty Bowman has demanded they do.

"I don't know if their intention is to lull anyone to sleep," Brendan Shanahan said. "That just may be the end result of playing good defense."

It does make for close contests in which the first team that scores two goals wins. The key for the Wings is to not get too annoyed. And not get distracted by the snoring.

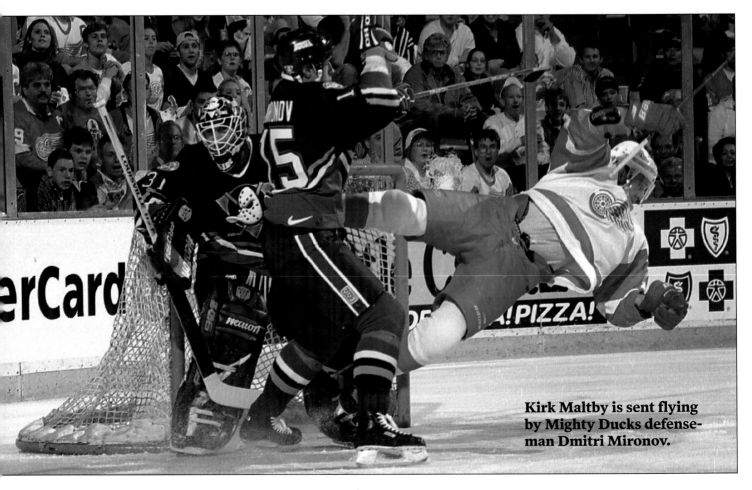

Kirk Maltby is sent flying by Mighty Ducks defenseman Dmitri Mironov.

KOZLOV HAS HUGE GAME

BY CYNTHIA LAMBERT

The Detroit News

GAME 2

Red Wings

3

Ducks

2

at Detroit
May 4, 1997

VYACHESLAV KOZLOV HAS A KNACK FOR SCORING HUGE goals in the playoffs.

He did it again Sunday night, scoring on the power play at 1:31 of the third overtime to give the Red Wings a 3-2 victory over the Mighty Ducks of Anaheim.

The Wings took a two-games-to-none lead in the best-of-seven series, with games 3 and 4 Tuesday and Thursday nights at The Pond.

"Scoring overtime goals is a great feeling," Kozlov said. "There were so many chances in the game. Both goalies played great."

Kozlov also had the series winner against Chicago in 1995. He scored at 2:25 of the second overtime to send the Wings to the Stanley Cup Finals.

Steve Yzerman and Doug Brown got the other Wings goals Sunday. Jari Kurri and Teemu Selanne scored for the Ducks.

But the goaltending was the real story. Anaheim used two goalies.

After starter Guy Hebert was lost to a groin injury at 7:02 of the third period, Mikhail Shtalenkov was outstanding in relief. The pair teamed for 68 saves.

At the other end, Mike Vernon was strong, playing the whole game and making 49 saves.

"I marvel at all goalies in the league," said the Wings' Scotty Bowman, who coached his first triple-overtime game. "This was the kind of game where the experience of the goalie is valuable. We had every confidence in Mike."

The Wings skaters were fairly sure they could beat Shtalenkov. But it took time. At 16:43 of the second overtime, Kozlov nearly scored.

Shtalenkov got enough of the puck to prevent the goal, but it still pinged off the left post.

"They got terrific goaltending," Bowman said. "We had some real good chances. They did, too, but we felt that if we kept taking it to them we would get it."

Despite having to switch goalies, Ducks Coach Ron Wilson said he had

Wings forward Vyacheslav Kozlov acknowledges the Joe Louis Arena fans after scoring the winning goal in the third overtime.

no reservations about Shtalenkov.

"I have every confidence in Mike," Wilson said. "You have to check if he has a pulse, he's so calm. You say, 'Mike, it's the last 10 minutes of the third, and we need you to go in.' He says, 'OK, Ron.' And he goes. He's one of the best relievers I've ever seen."

Whether the Wings see Shtalenkov in Game 3 remains to be seen.

After taking treatment for a couple of hours, Hebert said he felt better.

But at this rate, either one is a tough opponent for the Wings. But so far, they have the emotional edge and the 2-0 advantage.

"It's huge when you play almost two hockey games and don't come out with a win," Brendan Shanahan said. "I can imagine that's tough for them to deal with."

Despite two heartbreaking losses in overtime, Wilson said his team is still confident. The Ducks' ace in the hole is being on home ice, which helped them in the last series, against Phoenix. They won three of four games on home ice.

"We're not at all discouraged," Wilson said. "We're encouraged, actually. What we know is that they can't beat us in regulation. Now we go back to our building."

The Ducks appear to be feeding off their coach's beliefs and emotions. They, too, found positives in Sunday's game. And they vow to build on them beginning Tuesday night.

"We're not out of it," defenseman J.J. Daigneault said.

Redemption for Kozlov, Vernon

BY JERRY GREEN

The Detroit News

After 101-1/2 minutes of sometimes tense, sometimes blah playoff hockey, Vyacheslav Kozlov shot a puck at a target he couldn't see and scored a goal he never saw.

"I didn't see the net, and I didn't see the goal," Kozlov said. "I just got the puck, and I tried to snap it very hard, and I was surprised that it was in."

These dramatic sudden-death goals are becoming a specialty for Kozlov. Sunday night's winner at 1:31 of the third overtime enabled the Red Wings to defeat the Mighty Ducks and take command of their best-of-seven series, two games to none.

"What was the biggest goal you ever scored?" a reporter asked Kozlov.

"Two years ago I scored a double-overtime goal against Chicago," Kozlov said. "(The) Chicago series was different. We went to the Finals. Now we're only two games up.

"It's very positive."

The Russian realist.

The goal he scored two years ago enabled the Red Wings to eliminate the Blackhawks in five physically brutal games. He saw that one, skating through the middle and shooting. It came at 2:25 of the second overtime. And the Red Wings had been pounded so hard that they were swept by the Devils in the Finals.

In the aftermath of the 1995 Stanley Cup Finals, Detroit's hockey fans turned against goalkeeper Mike Vernon. He was booed last season and lost his No. 1 status to Chris Osgood. It wasn't until March that he regained his standing, with the fans and, more important, with Coach Scotty Bowman.

And Sunday, the fans broke into the chant of "Vernie, Vernie, Vernie" four times after Vernon foiled the Ducks on breakaways.

Vernon was the game-saver for the Red Wings in the first overtime.

Early in the period, the Ducks' Warren Rychel and Mark Janssens broke in on Vernon. He saved a goal on his knees, grabbing the puck in his trapper. He twice stopped Paul Kariya, first on a breakaway and then on a quick shot following a faceoff. He beat Steve Rucchin close in. Then he foiled Bobby Dollas' shot from the point, and turned away the rebound from Sean Pronger at the edge of the crease.

In all, Vernon made 49 saves.

Funny, Vernon and Kozlov had been benched by Bowman during the season and were subjects of those trade rumors that annually float around the Red Wings. "You need that goaltending," said Bowman, who has not had to use his goaltenders mysteriously in this year's playoffs.

Vernon has started all seven of the Red Wings' playoff games. And Bowman spoke in admiration of goaltenders.

Wings goalie Mike Vernon, who made 49 saves, stops Sean Pronger.

"All that equipment to put on, and to have a small puck that goes 100 miles an hour," he said. "It's a unique job."

The Wings are headed for Anaheim for games 3 and 4 of this Western Conference series and are in a fine position. Historically, teams that win the Stanley Cup emerge from the pack of regular-season finishers. The best of the regular-season teams, for some reason, are eliminated. Six of the last seven teams that finished first in the regular season did not win the Stanley Cup. Such as the Red Wings were last season and the year before.

"It wasn't by design," said Bowman, whose team, which finished third in the Western Conference, is soaring.

RED WINGS RALLY FROM 2-0 DEFICIT

BY CYNTHIA LAMBERT

The Detroit News

SOMETIMES, THE BEST ENDINGS COME FROM THE WORST BEGINNINGS.

The Red Wings had one of those nights Tuesday. They got in trouble early because of penalties and trailed 2-0 by 12:09 of the first period.

GAME 3

Red Wings

5

Ducks

3

**at Anaheim
May 6, 1997**

But they rebounded to defeat the Mighty Ducks of Anaheim, 5-3, at the Pond to take a three-games-to-none lead in the best-of-seven Western Conference semifinal series.

"Despite the start we had ... we were skating hard," Brendan Shanahan said. "We seemed to elevate our game with each shift."

The Wings can clinch the series with a victory in Game 4 on Thursday night at Anaheim and advance to the conference finals for the third straight season. The last time the Wings swept a series was in 1995, when they defeated the San Jose Sharks in the second round.

"It was a tough game for us, especially in the beginning," Igor Larionov said. "We knew before the game that we

The Wings celebrate one of their five goals in Game 3.

The Ducks' Jason Marshall tries to bring down Tomas Sandstrom.

had a chance to be up 3-0 and we decided we really wanted to play well."

Those plans were nearly derailed midway through the first period when the Wings took three straight minor penalties to give the Ducks two 5-on-3 advantages. They connected on both with goals by Paul Kariya and Teemu Selanne.

Vyacheslav Kozlov got a power-play goal at 15:47 of the first to make it 2-1. Ted Drury scored at 5:12 of the second to give the Ducks a 3-1 lead.

But it also was the end of their offense.

Larionov (power play) and Doug Brown scored to make it 3-3 after two periods. Goals by Sergei Fedorov and Kozlov in a 24-second span early in the third gave the Wings the padding they needed.

"We had gotten ourselves into penalty trouble early," Brown said.

"But there was so much hockey left at that point, there was no pessimism."

Two teams have rallied from a 3-0 deficit to win a series: Toronto, in1943, against the Red Wings; and the New York Islanders, in 1975, against the Penguins.

"I know this, there's going to be a third (someday)," Ducks forward Brian Bellows said. "And hopefully, it'll be the Ducks."

Vernon overcomes temper tantrum

BY CYNTHIA LAMBERT

The Detroit News

Mike Vernon didn't need anyone to tell him that he lost it. He admitted as much.

And when the Wings' 5-3 victory was over, he thanked his teammates for overcoming his show of anger and frustration midway through the first period that helped Anaheim to a 2-0 lead.

It all started at 9:34, when Vladimir Konstantinov was called for tripping Richard Park, a call the Wings contested and Vernon couldn't believe. About a minute later, Vernon was called for high sticking, which he hotly contested, claiming Paul Kariya ran into him.

With the Ducks about to start their first of two 5-on-3 situations, Vernon skated over to referee Bill McCreary and gave him a piece of his mind. McCreary listened for a while. When he had enough, he tacked on a 10-minute misconduct for Vernon, a penalty served by Doug Brown.

"I cost Dougie Brown the Lady Byng," said Vernon, referring to the award given for gentmanly conduct on the ice.

"There was no doubt, it put us in a hole. In the course of a game, we're going to take some penalties, but that put us in a hole. I thanked the guys after for coming back."

Coach Scotty Bowman attempted to calm Vernon down after the misconduct by calling him over to the bench. After a few words, Vernon was back in the net.

Wings Coach Scotty Bowman tries to calm down goalie Mike Vernon in the first period.

Anaheim is casualty when Russian Five, led by Larionov, Fedorov, go duck hunting

By Bob Wojnowski

The Detroit News

Advice to Ducks and anyone else thinking of skating with the Red Wings' Russians: Don't.

The Ducks, still young, still foolish, made the colossal mistake of riling the Wings, then trying to outskate them. With a flurry we hadn't seen in a while, Detroit rolled to a 5-3 victory over Anaheim, all but sealing its Western Conference semifinal series with a three-games-to-none lead.

First, the Ducks got chippy while building a 2-0 edge. Then, their fans got chirpy, chanting "USA! USA!" at the Russian unit.

By the end, after two goals by Slava Kozlov, one by Igor Larionov and one by Sergei Fedorov, Anaheim limped off with its (duck) tail between its legs.

"We played simple Russian hockey," Larionov said. "We moved the puck, we skated well. But I don't think we should just talk about our unit. Everyone played well."

Maybe so. But this was a night for the Russians, who made Anaheim's tiring, mistake-prone defense pay dearly. After Kozlov sliced the Ducks' lead with his first goal, the chants quieted, even as Slava Fetisov waved his arms, asking for more. When Larionov tipped in a Kozlov shot, the chants died. When Fedorov and Kozlov scored 24 seconds apart in the third period to break a 3-3 tie, it was so quiet at The Pond, you could hear a Duck quack.

This is how dangerous the Wings can be, especially when facing a back-up goalie in Mikhail Shtalenkov. This is what makes the five-man Russian unit intriguing, even though it had combined for only four goals in eight playoff games before Tuesday night. It can break open a murky series with puck control and domination you seldom see.

"Igor's the glue to that line, and they're back having fun," Darren McCarty said. "When they get Sergei going, they're unstoppable. They feed off each other."

Fedorov's goal 3:34 into the third period came amid a blur of skating that left the Ducks dizzy, even daffy. The Wings outshot Anaheim 23-6 in the second period, finished with a 49-23 edge and might have scored 10 goals if they hadn't dawdled early, logging a succession of miscues.

Referee Bill McCreary apparently heard Ducks Coach Ron Wilson talk about the Wings' "dirty" tactics and blew his whistle with impunity. Paul Kariya and Teemu Selanne each scored on two-man advantages and Mike Vernon appeared to rattle after getting a high-sticking penalty.

Once they regained their composure, they never lost it. And really, this is the difference in these Wings. If a game turns ugly, they can handle it. If Vernon struggles, they don't reel. If a team abandons its defense and tries to skate with the Wings, they'll skate 'em to death.

"It's just a matter of time," Fetisov said. "I kept telling the guys to be patient, sooner or later, we'll score. We kept digging, not complaining."

Not even amid those silly "USA!" chants from Duck fans too stupid to realize a Russian was tending their own net.

"If they think they can get us off our game," Fetisov said, smiling, "they're probably wrong." Kozlov, tops on the team with five playoff goals, has his confidence back. So does Fedorov. For the Ducks, icing the puck was a minor victory. Even when they led, it was like a triple-scoop ice cream cone -- looks good, sure to melt.

It melted under the speed and relentless of the Wings' flashiest players. The crowd sat in silence, maybe awe, as the Wings applied constant pressure. Really, the next inspirational movie Wilson should show his team is From Russia, With Love.

Perhaps the Wings were riled by the early scrums. Maybe they were just superior and needed time to prove it. The Russians were flying and the Ducks were moving as if their skates were webbed. It was something to behold, but the Ducks shouldn't fret. They only have to see it one more game.

WINGS GIVE DUCKS THE BRUSH OFF IN DOUBLE OT

Shanahan's goal ends the series

BY CYNTHIA LAMBERT

The Detroit News

DOUG BROWN CALLED IT A SIX-GAME SWEEP. HE WASN'T FAR OFF.

The Red Wings, getting a goal from Brendan Shanahan 17:03 into the second overtime period, defeated the Mighty Ducks of Anaheim, 3-2, Thursday night to reach the Western Conference finals for the third consecutive season.

The Wings took the Ducks in four straight games, but it seemed like more because only one was decided in regulation. The other three went into one, two and three overtimes.

"We kept saying that we played more overtime games than any other team," a grinning Shanahan said. "I think that was good preparation for this."

During the regular season, the Wings played overtime 27 out of 82 times, going 7-2-18.

"We were fortunate when it was over," Wings Coach Scotty Bowman said. "We actually played 5-1/2 or six games. We knew if they won, they would get a big lift out of a game like this."

It was, at the same time, a long and short series. But the game didn't start with that look, because the Ducks jumped early. Anaheim took a 1-0 lead on Joe Sacco's goal at 3:01 of the first. But Brown tied it at 18:25 when he scored his third goal in four playoff games.

Brian Bellows (power play) restored the Ducks lead at

GAME 4

Red Wings

3

Ducks

2

at Anaheim
May 8, 1997

15:23 of the second period, a lead that held until Nick Lidstrom scored his first of the playoffs at 9:09 of the third.

"It was a tough series," Igor Larionov said. "We had three overtime games, and two of them were long ones. That's almost six games. We had so many great chances in this game in overtime to finish the series, but the puck didn't want to go to the net. Shanny got his chance, and he scored."

Shanahan's goal was his first of the series and came on his eighth shot of the game. During the flurry around goalie Mikhail Shtalenkov, the puck popped loose and Shanahan was there, at the right edge of the crease, to shoot it in.

"Your instincts take over at that point," Shanahan said. "Warren Rychel and I collided, and he fell into their guys, and it opened a (lane) for me. The puck just popped out, and I got it."

**Brendan Shanahan gets a hug
from Vyacheslav Kozlov after
scoring the winner.**

Wings relentless to outlast the Ducks

BY BOB WOJNOWSKI

The Detroit News

It's a simple lesson of hockey: Keep shooting until you find the target.

The Red Wings fired and fired and fired (and fired and fired) at the Anaheim Sitting Ducks, past regulation, past the first overtime, past 3 a.m. Detroit time, into the second overtime, into that dangerous area where persistence melts to frustration.

The Wings kept firing, kept plugging, and because they did, they move on. Brendan Shanahan, brought to Detroit to score the grit goals, slammed in a rebound 17:03 into the second overtime to give the Wings a 3-2 victory and a series sweep that was harder than it should have been, easier than the score indicated.

The Wings never let up, which is all they could do. They dominated play, peppering goalie Mikhail Shtalenkov with 73 shots and probably another two dozen that went high or wide. In the end, the Wings simply overwhelmed the Ducks, win-

The Mighty Ducks' Dan Trebil keeps Wings' Kris Draper pinned to the ice.

ning their third overtime game of the series to advance to the Western Conference finals for the third straight year.

"It showed our experience and savvy, to play in these situations and be so assertive and aggressive," said Shanahan, who also scored the winner in the clinching Game 6 against St. Louis. "On the bench and in the dressing room, everyone was calm. Looking back to the triple-overtime (victory in Game 2), we didn't press

and start taking shortcuts."

No shortcuts for this team, which even had to wait through a video review of the winning goal. When referee Kerry Fraser signaled it good, goalie Mike Vernon (again, the overlooked hero) leaped and kicked one leg as fans in the half-empty Pond clapped slowly in appreciation.

This was about persistence, about the new-look Wings not caving under the pressure of a nasty duckfight. They won their sixth straight playoff

Anaheim goaltender Mikhail Shtalenkov keeps Vyacheslav Kozlov from crossing the crease.

game, and we hypemeisters can hardly wait to see if they face Colorado.

Of course, the Wings cannot count on their overtime magic continuing, so they are advised to spend time in target practice, with extra work for Shanahan, Steve Yzerman and Igor Larionov. Much of this game was a microcosm of the series — stretches of nothing interrupted by skating exhibitions by the Wings, who did what they do best, creating chances, tons of them. The Ducks did what

they do best, waiting for chances, hanging on. The Wings outshot Anaheim, 73-37, and were every bit that dominant.

"We couldn't get uptight," said Yzerman, who missed a golden chance in the first overtime. "When you're getting that many chances, you just keep with what you're doing."

The Ducks stayed admirably plucky, largely because the Wings permitted them to do so. At some point (like in the next round against a tougher foe), the Wings must finish their chances and close out games before, say, 3 a.m. To their credit, they didn't let up, they just didn't line up their shots very well, except for Doug Brown, the seldom-used regular-season forward who scored his third goal in four post-season games.

Shanahan got the winner, but it

could have been anyone, because everyone had a whack at winning it. The bad thing is, most of the chances went awry. The good thing is, the Wings just sent out another line and fired more.

"We have a lot of guys on this team who want to be the hero," Shanahan said. "I love those moments. I'm the one who asked to come here, and I'm so thrilled to be here. I owe this to the city and the team."

Shanahan needed that goal, his first of the series, his fourth of the playoffs. The Wings needed that goal to get more than a week of rest before the next round. Bleary-eyed residents of Detroit needed that goal, to move on with their lives.

The lesson of the game and the series? Keep firing, but aim a little better. The target gets considerably tougher.

CONFERENCE
FINALS

DRAPER: 'WE COULDN'T BURY' SCORING CHANCES

BY CYNTHIA LAMBERT

The Detroit News

MIKE RICCI'S GOAL, his second of the playoffs, allowed the Colorado Avalanche to draw first blood against the Red Wings with a 2-1 victory Thursday night in Game 1 of the Western Conference finals.

The game was as hard-hitting and antagonistic as expected. But more

Colorado's Sandis Ozolinsh gets in the face of Tomas Sandstrom, who is closing on Patrick Roy in the first period.

than anything, it was a game the Wings might look back on as one they could have won, maybe should have won.

"No one's going to hang their heads after this one," Kris Draper said. "We had our chances but we couldn't bury them."

It seems to be a recurring theme for the Wings in the postseason. But in the previous two series, they scored after

drastically outshooting their opponent. On Thursday night, when they needed a goal, they couldn't get it.

After an evenly played first period, the Wings carried the play in the second, outshooting the Avalanche, 13-2. Colorado went 14 minutes without a shot on goal in the second period. But the Wings couldn't convert on their chances and the game was scoreless

GAME 1

Red Wings

1

Avalanche

2

at Colorado
May 15, 1997

Mike Vernon at 1:40 to tie the score at 1.

Ricci's goal, at 6:13, gave the Avalanche the lead. Ricci and Claude Lemieux broke in with only Martin Lapointe back after two Wings went to cover Sakic. Lemieux, cutting wide around the right circle, passed across to Ricci, who snapped a shot into the left side of the net.

"After we got the 1-0 lead, it seemed like we sat back a bit," Shanahan said. "On the Ricci goal, they broke into our zone pretty easily. But I think we played a sound game defensively. It looks like it's going to be great goaltending that's going to be the difference in this series."

The Avalanche said they didn't play their best game, but goalie Patrick Roy was outstanding.

"We weren't happy with the way we played the first two periods," Avalanche forward Eric Lacroix said. "We kind of sat back a little. We only had 10 shots. It's just not enough. We addressed it and I thought we played a solid third period."

The Wings had several chances in the third to tie the score and force overtime. One was at 13:07, when Sylvain Lefebvre was penalized for elbowing Igor Larionov. The Wings threatened on the power play, taking three shots. But they couldn't beat Roy, who has allowed seven goals in seven home playoff games, all won by the Avalanche.

"We had our chances," defenseman Larry Murphy said. "It feels like you let it slip away when you have those kind of chances. We played well, but we didn't capitalize on our opportunities. It was a game that could have gone either way. But it was tough because we had some really good chances."

Part of the problem might have been poor ice conditions. Before the game, a power failure possibly caused by thunderstorms rendered two chillers that cool the ice inoperable for about 90 minutes.

By the end of the second period, puddles of water lay on the ice surface. Where heaps of snow generally pile up near the nets, there was slush.

Although each team had to play on the surface, Shanahan said the advantage went to the Avalanche.

"I kind of thought the ice affected things late in the game, when we were trying to catch up," Shanahan said. "A couple of times I noticed when the puck was shot in, it was bouncing around with the bad ice. When you've got bad ice like that, you want the lead."

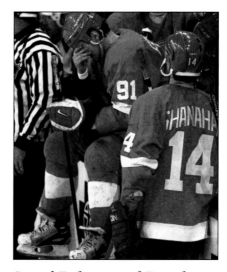

Sergei Fedorov and Brendan Shanahan must regroup after losing Game 1.

entering the third.

That ended quickly when Brendan Shanahan scored at 1:13, just as a Wings' power play ended.

The Avalanche gave the Wings fair warning they wouldn't fold when a backhand shot by Valeri Kamensky clanged off the left post and Joe Sakic followed with a shot off the crossbar.

On the next play, Sakic beat goalie

CAPTAIN KEYS COMEBACK

BY CYNTHIA LAMBERT

The Detroit News

SCOTTY BOWMAN POUNDED ON THE LEDGE IN FRONT OF THE RED WINGS'

GAME 2
Red Wings **Avs**
4 **2**
at Colorado May 17, 1997

bench and allowed a tight grin.

On the ice, Claude Lemieux smashed his stick over a crossbar, curled his upper lip and spat hot remarks at referee Don Koharski.

One was gratified, the other outraged. Both were representative of their team's sentiments after the Red Wings rallied from a two-goal deficit to defeat the Colorado Avalanche, 4-2, Saturday night in the Western Conference finals.

A diving Adam Foote can't stop Darren McCarty from beating Patrick Roy for Wings' fourth goal.

The best-of-seven series is tied at a game apiece.

Red Wings captain Steve Yzerman scored the winner at 16:00 of the third period, and Darren McCarty followed with a breakaway goal with 1:27 to preserve the victory. It was the first loss in eight home playoff games this year for the Avalanche. It was the fourth time in the playoffs this year that the Wings have come back to win after trailing entering the third period.

"This was the deepest down we've had to dig so far to get this win," forward Brendan Shanahan said.

And it likely was the most gratifying.

"We knew we could compete with his hockey club," said goalie Mike Vernon, who made 15 saves. "We had chances early, but, like he did in the first game, (Patrick) Roy robbed us. We started to wonder if it was going to be another case of hot goaltending.

"But what the guys showed tonight is that they weren't going to be satisfied with just saying we ran into a hot goalie."

But as the game wore on, there wouldn't have been many who could blame the Wings if they did.

By 16:09 of the second, the Wings trailed 2-0 on goals by Scott Young (power play) and Lemieux. Each goal was scored after the Wings had dominated play.

With the Wings on their fourth power play at 16:51 of the second, Igor Larionov banked a shot off Adam Foote's stick, sending the puck high over Roy's glove and into the net to give the Wings the break they needed.

"I thought the key was Igor's goal, coming when it did, late in the second," Yzerman said.

The Wings built on that momentum, and at 2:10 of the third Sergei Fedorov got a power-play goal after a nice setup by Yzerman. Roy preserved the tie at 3:22 when he made a diving save on a Vyacheslav Kozlov shot that seemed almost a sure goal.

But by that time, the Roy mystery had been solved. At 16:00, Yzerman went behind the net, and banked the puck off the back of Roy's legs and into the net to give the Wings the lead.

McCarty converted on a breakaway for the insurance goal. McCarty's approach to the net and the ease with which he scored belied his emotions.

"Relaxed?" McCarty said. "That's not how I felt."

"We didn't play a strong game," Coach Marc Crawford said. "I think the guys are trying, but they're trying in different directions. They're not working together."

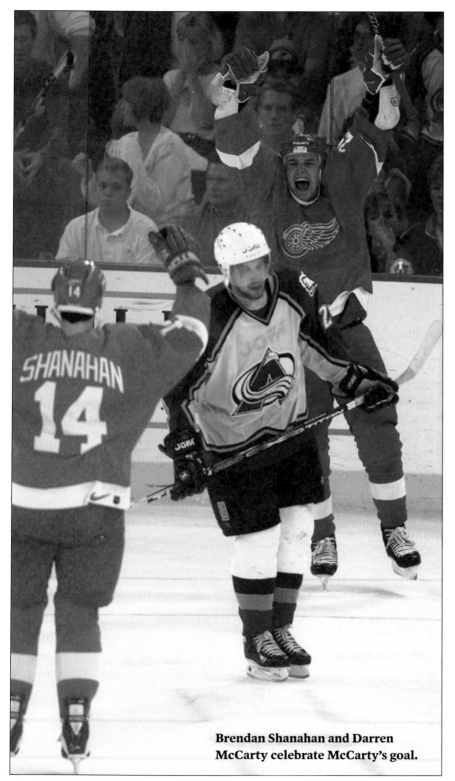

Brendan Shanahan and Darren McCarty celebrate McCarty's goal.

Wings finally get through vs. Avs' Roy

BY BOB WOJNOWSKI

The Detroit News

Just keep shooting. They said it between periods, between shifts, on the bench, in the dressing room. Just keep shooting, that was the Red Wings' mantra, and by the end of a stunning onslaught, it was their message, delivered 40 times, tattooed on Patrick Roy's mask.

This wasn't a game, it was target practice, and all night long, the Wings cocked, fired, reloaded ... cocked, fired, reloaded. Finally, after relentless attacking, they solved Roy and shocked Colorado 4-2 to knot the Western Conference finals at 1.

This is the way you win big games, with your stars showing up and refusing to be denied. Even after the Avs built a 2-0 lead, even after Roy seemed capable of stopping every puck, the Wings never, ever relented, led by their captain.

Steve Yzerman banked the winning goal off Roy's back with four minutes left, sweet success for a team that dominated the Avs, outshooting them 40-17. Darren McCarty clinched it with a breakaway goal in the closing minutes. Sergei Fedorov broke out of a scoring slump with the tying goal 2:10 into the third period.

"You just stick with it, there's nothing else you can do," said Yzerman, who played brilliantly. "We believe in ourselves. We got stronger as it went along, spending more time in their end of the rink."

Detroit is home for Game 3 Monday night, armed with loads of momentum, Colorado's veneer of invincibility sheared away. Roy will have nightmares of rubber orbs whistling toward him — in two games, the Wings outshot the Avs 75-36 and finally showed signs of solving their playoff scoring woes.

"We never got discouraged, we just pushed harder," Wings' Coach Scotty Bowman said. "I told our guys that we were worrying the other team, so just keep playing."

The Wings did, with a performance that was equal parts grit, composure and skill. Centers Yzerman, Fedorov and Igor Larionov controlled play and kept the defending champions skating backward all night.

Roy became the focal point, and more than Claude Lemieux, he's the one who could have crawled inside the Wings' heads. Now, after their remarkable turnaround, they might have climbed into his. Certainly, they chipped away at the mental wall Roy was erecting, save by save. And they flustered plastic-haired Avs Coach Marc Crawford, who was a bit testy after the game.

"We're not mystified by it, we were awful," Crawford said. "When you play as individuals, against a strong puck-possession team like the Red Wings, they burn you."

The Wings' offense became a stifling defense, holding Avs star Joe Sakic without a single shot. Peter Forsberg and Mike Ricci got one each as Mike Vernon again was rarely tested, but passed most of them.

In a strange flip, it was the Avs who grew frustrated, and for a while, they looked like Anaheim all over again. One team (the Wings) swarmed; the other (Anaheim, or Colorado) tried to hang on.

Just like in the opener, the Wings threw the puck at Roy. You want the perfect snapshot, here it is: Early in the second period, Fedorov picks the puck off the boards and fires it at Roy, who kicks it to the front of the net. For the next five seconds, Brendan Shanahan, Doug Brown and Larry Murphy take turns swatting at it, as if playing Whack-a-Mole at the state fair.

Midway through the second period, Martin Lapointe, who has played well, flipped a backhand at Roy that we're certain he never saw, but kicked away out of reflex. The Wings pressured on almost every possession, and when you do that, good things happen eventually, don't they?

They do if you're persistent, and insistent. When the Wings solved Roy, they did it with a ricochet, one of two power-play goals. Larionov bounced it off defenseman Adam Foote at 16:51 of the second period, shaving Colorado's lead to 2-1.

All you can do is keep shooting, keep skating, and hope Roy turns beatable before it's too late. Finally, when they could wait no longer, the Wings' stars showed up, took over and never let up. We believe Mr. Roy received the message.

The Wings' Darren McCarty, who scored the game's final goal, makes his presence felt against Eric Messier in the first period.

COMMAND PERFORMANCE

By Cynthia Lambert

The Detroit News

Vyacheslav Kozlov knew exactly where the puck went, but because it bounced out of the net as quickly as it went in, play continued, even though the goal judge turned on the red light to signify a goal.

GAME 3

Red Wings

2

Avalanche

1

at Detroit
May 19, 1997

It wasn't until moments later, after referee Kerry Fraser confirmed it with the video-replay judge, that Kozlov's goal was posted on the scoreboard at Joe Louis Arena.

"I saw it," said Kozlov, who scored twice in the Red Wings' 2-1 victory over the Colorado Avalanche on Monday night in Game 3 of the Western Conference finals.

"I saw it was in," he said. "And then I saw Kerry Fraser and he knew, too.

I saw it go in and hit the second cross-bar, in the net."

The goal — Kozlov's second winner of the playoffs — came at 8:20 of the third period. It was his second of the game and team-best seventh of the postseason, and not only gave the Wings the victory, but also a two-games-to-one lead in the best-of-seven series. Game 4 is Thursday night at Joe Louis Arena.

"I didn't have much doubt," Wings Coach Scotty Bowman said. "The players on the ice knew it was in. Doug Brown came over and said it was good. And I trust Doug Brown."

After Monday night, Bowman should have more faith in the Wings' penalty-killing and in Mike

Vernon, who made 27 saves in a superb performance.

Bowman said he has never seen Vernon play better. Colorado Coach Marc Crawford said Vernon was a key.

"He kept them in the game," Crawford said. "Vernon was great tonight. He gave his team a chance to get into the game. He persevered and stayed strong for them. He was the difference in the early part of the game."

Said Sergei Fedorov: "He meant everything to us. We won because of Mike Vernon. He stood up like a wall."

If not for Vernon, the Wings would have been in deep trouble in the first period. Although Kozlov's first goal, at 1:12 of the first, gave the Wings a 1-0 lead, the momentum dwindled after

Overlooked Goalie Keeps Detroit in Game to Net Series Lead

BY BOB WOJNOWSKI

The Detroit News

Colorado Goalie Patrick Roy goes a long way from home to clear the puck before the Wings' Brendan Shanahan arrives.

each of three Wings penalties. Two were called on Martin Lapointe and one on Darren McCarty in a span of 5:32. But the Avalanche did not score, and went 1-for-5 with the man-advantage overall.

"We watched the tape and I don't think we'll get five next game," Bowman said. "We lost our focus a bit. We lost more, our energy, taking three in succession."

The Avalanche totaled nine shots on the three first-period power plays. On two, Vernon made breathtaking saves, including one that left him a little breathless.

It came at 9:45, when Colorado shot the puck along the right boards and behind the Detroit net. Vernon came out on the left side to intercept the puck, but it careened high into the slot to Adam Deadmarsh, who fired it to the left side of the net. Vernon was quick enough to pounce on the puck before it crossed the goal line.

"It hit one of the metal things on the glass and went right out in front," Vernon said. "I tried to get back as quick as I could. I don't think he got good wood on the shot."

But the Wings had to knock on wood after the save because they could have lost their lead. They would lose it at 14:47 of the second, when Joe Sakic scored a power-play goal to make it 1-1. Kozlov's second goal put the Wings ahead to stay. The Avalanche pulled goalie Patrick Roy for an extra attacker with 1:04 remaining, but they couldn't get the equalizer.

The Avalanche played their best game of the series, and Crawford said they must play the same way, or better, Thursday night.

"We played a lot better tonight, but we need to get everybody going and tonight we had probably three-quarters of the guys going at the level we have to," Crawford said. "We need the other quarter of the guys going. And when we get that, that's what it's going to take to solve the Red Wings."

Minute by minute, save by save, Mike Vernon held on and held held off the attackers, kicking away pucks, leaping at pucks, diving at pucks. Sometimes, in the Stanley Cup playoffs, you need everyone playing superbly. Sometimes, you only need one.

When the Red Wings had to have him, when the defending champion Avalanche finally announced their arrival in this Western Conference final, Vernon announced his. On a night of sweaty-palmed grit, he would not fold, and barely even blinked.

The score sheet will say the Wings beat Colorado, 2-1, Monday night to take a 2-1 series lead because Vyacheslav Kozlov scored twice, the winning goal at 8:20 into the third period. But the Wings reached that point because Vernon delivered them there, continuing the postseason's longest-running irony.

Vernon was trade bait until February, when Scotty Bowman

finally told him he'd be around. Then Bowman told him he'd be in net for the playoffs. Monday, the strange ascent continued, with Bowman saying the 27-save performance was the best he'd ever seen by Vernon.

Vernon shrugged, smiled and savored the irony.

"That's nice to hear, but I hope I still have a lot left," he said. "Maybe it was good for me that I didn't play much early in the season. It let me boil inside for awhile."

Oh, he's boiling now, and this morning the Avs must be scratching and wondering how many weapons the Wings possess, and when Vernon's run will end. He's 10-3 with a 1.80 goals-against average, yet everyone seems to be waiting for the dam to break. Vernon doesn't talk as brashly as his counterpart, Patrick Roy, and sounds like a guy who knows how quickly it can turn.

"You don't get too many opportunities in your career, and when you do, you have to seize it," he said. "I'm just trying to hold up my end of the bargain."

Vernon hung on until someone could win it, and someone did — the lonely sniper, Kozlov, who fired a shot that Roy might see if he watches the highlights. As long as it was Retribution Night at the Joe, Kozlov continued to get his. Also on the trading block at one point, Kozlov leads the team with seven playoff goals.

It was as if Vernon gave Kozlov and the Wings reason to keep firing. In the first period, he made three spectacular stops, including one on Adam Deadmarsh that foreshadowed the night. The puck bounced behind the net, where Vernon chased it, before it caromed crazily in front. Deadmarsh, all alone, slid it toward the goal ...

until Vernon popped it back, reached low and scooped it.

"Vernie won the game for us," Darren McCarty said. "Hopefully, we won't have to bank on him every night., but he was there when we needed him."

He had been there before, winning a Cup with Calgary in 1989, taking the Wings to the finals two years ago. For too long, Vernon, 34, has been overlooked and underestimated. He's a free agent after this season so he's driven by forces more powerful than we know.

This series was supposed to be about the other goalie, but then, Vernon is accustomed to the slight, and maybe even relishes it. Because the Wings insisted on taking dumb penalties, the Avs had three power plays in the first period and put the puck everywhere but in the net. Valeri Kamensky even raised his arms to celebrate an apparent goal that Vernon had kicked wide.

To win it all, your goalie eventually must swipe a game, and this was

Vernon's, against a Colorado team fuming about its lackluster play. If these Wings are Team Resilience, Vernon is their mascot. He won't rattle, and maybe this is the year the Wings don't roll (over).

"Vernon gave his team a chance to get into the game," Avs coach Marc Crawford said. "He persevered and stayed strong."

This was different from the first two games, when the Wings outshot the Avs, 75-36. The Avalanche finally were the team we expected, the haughty champ. If not for Vernon, Colorado would have taken command. Of course, if not for Roy, the Wings would have won twice in Denver.

As these teams shake off the nerves and remember how much they hate each other, it will become a goaltender's series. On this night, the Avs kept shooting until they saw the red in Vernon's eyes. It was a look of confidence, an old familiar look, one that suddenly makes the Wings seem far more formidable.

Goalie Mike Vernon did anything he could to see the puck, which he was able to do most of the time for the Red Wings.

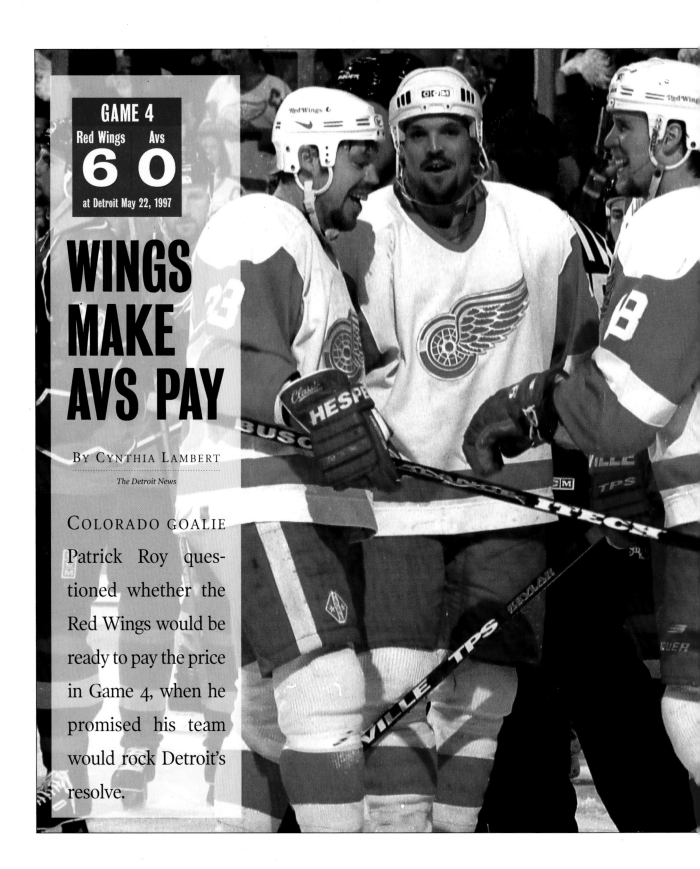

GAME 4

Red Wings | Avs

6 0

at Detroit May 22, 1997

WINGS MAKE AVS PAY

BY CYNTHIA LAMBERT
....
The Detroit News

COLORADO GOALIE Patrick Roy questioned whether the Red Wings would be ready to pay the price in Game 4, when he promised his team would rock Detroit's resolve.

The Wings made Roy's words seem dreadfully miscalculated and downright silly as they slammed the answer back in his face — a handful of times — on the way to a 6-0 victory at Joe Louis Arena.

Entering Game 5 Saturday night in Denver, the Wings lead the best-of-seven Western Conference finals, three games to one.

Roy, who was pulled after two periods, said the Avalanche played "stupid." His teammates agreed.

"We got embarrassed pretty bad tonight," Adam Deadmarsh said.

Embarrassed, outplayed, outsmarted and outscored. The Wings return to Denver with the chance to close the series and advance to the Stanley Cup Finals for the second time in three years.

"There is no way we ever expected this kind of game to happen," Wings defenseman Larry Murphy said. "It wasn't by design, I'll tell you. All of a sudden we were up by a pile of goals. The trick now is to remember it was just one game. We have to keep our heads on straight."

Game 5 will be a test of whether the Avalanche and Coach Marc Crawford can keep their heads cooler than they were Thursday. After the Wings took their big lead, the play turned ugly late in the third period.

One of the ugliest incidents occurred with 2:18 to play, when a number of fights broke out, including one between Brendan Shanahan and Rene Corbet. Shanahan bloodied Corbet,

Kris Draper, left, Joe Kocur, center, Kirk Maltby and the Wings showed the Avalanche how much actions speak louder than words.

who had to be helped off the ice.

Shortly thereafter, Crawford stood on the Avalanche bench and began shouting at Wings Coach Scotty Bowman. Crawford was restrained by his players, and Bowman remained calm. Linesman Gord Broseker had to jump into the Detroit bench area to keep the teams apart.

"He said he got one of our players," Bowman said. "I think he was referring to Igor (Larionov). I told him, 'It's a hockey game.' His eyes were coming out of his head. He was pretty emotional."

While the Avalanche personified high emotion, the Wings were composed. The Avalanche paid the price for the unruly behavior as the Wings had 13 power plays and scored twice with the man-advantage.

The Avalanche didn't go on a power play until the Wings led 2-0.

Larionov opened the scoring with a power-play goal at 1:52 of the first. He centered a pass that deflected off the stick of Avalanche defenseman Alexei Gusarov and into the net. Larionov got his second goal at 7:15 of the first when he beat Roy with a backhand shot.

The Wings' key goal came in the second period, shortly after they held the Avalanche without a shot on their second power play. Vyacheslav Kozlov, who was penalized for cross-checking Corbet, left the penalty box just as Sergei Fedorov chipped the puck into the neutral zone. Kozlov was on a breakaway, and he faked right, then went high left on Roy to make it 3-0.

"When Kozlov scored to make it 3-0, that was a big swing," Bowman said.

Fedorov scored a power-play goal and Maltby scored twice to complete the rout.

Brendan Shanahan skates away after knocking out Rene Corbet in the third period. The Wings floored the Avs, 6-0.

"Tonight, we obviously didn't respond," Crawford said. "We're not proud of the way we performed. They scored on the power play right away and that put us back on our heels. It seemed like we were killing penalties for the entire first period. You lick your wounds and try to come back and win the next one."

The Avalanche must do that for three straight games if they want a chance to repeat as Stanley Cup champions. But they are facing a team with loads of momentum.

"Whatever you think, our hockey club showed we can do something right," said Wings goalie Mike Vernon, who made 19 saves for his first playoff shutout this year and fifth of his career.

"What we showed is that we are believers in ourselves," Vernon said.

"And we're getting better and better. I think everybody was outstanding tonight."

Red Wings reduce the Avs to ashes

BY BOB WOJNOWSKI

The Detroit News

They hit with everything, from every direction, in every possible way. The Russians scored and the agitators agitated and the fighters fought, and by the end of the game Thursday night, the Red Wings had struck with such ferocity, with such perfect clarity, the Avalanche was left to flail and wail in pathetic frustration, as defeated as a team can look.

With dizzying dominance and ridiculous ease, the Wings toyed with Colorado and turned their Western Conference finals into a battle between the Haves and the Av-nots. Don't be fooled by the score — 6-0, Wings. It wasn't nearly that close, or that simple.

The Avs lost total composure, led by their smarmy coach, Marc Crawford. In the closing minutes, after Brendan Shanahan had pounded Colorado's Rene Corbet, Crawford screamed at Scotty Bowman and tried furiously to yank out a pane of glass between the benches. It was the final ugly act in a game that began with Detroit dominance and ended in bloody bitterness, and it wonderfully reflected the teams.

On one side of the glass, Crawford yelled, "I'm going to kick your little (bleeping) (butt)!" This, according to the cameraman caught in the middle.

Bowman listened intently and said little, his expression unchanging, as unflappable as his team.

Oh, the Avs can talk. They just can't score. Or keep their cool. Or handle the heat. And barring a monumental turnaround, they can't beat the Wings in this series. The Wings waited a year for this opportunity and they shouldn't have to wait much longer to finish it. In a performance as remarkable as any we've seen in Joe Louis Arena, Detroit seized a three-games-to-one lead, one victory from the Stanley Cup finals.

The Wings have done the unthinkable, reducing the defending champs to emotional ashes. If the Avs piece themselves together after this humiliating surrender, it would be one of the great patch jobs in NHL history.

The third period deteriorated into a succession of brawls as old emotions bubbled over. Trying to get players to discuss the cause was virtually impossible, as both teams switched into stoic mode afterward. But Colorado's Mike Keane did send Igor Larionov, who had scored twice, to the dressing room with a slash midway through the period. Larionov has a calf contusion, and his status was unknown.

"I guess they felt whatever they were doing prior wasn't working, so they figured they'd try something else," Wings defenseman Bob Rouse said. "I thought we kept pretty disciplined, for the most part."

Keane, who has accused the Wings of being "gutless and heartless," showed the Avs to be gutless, heartless and brainless. On that last matter, on this night, they pleaded guilty.

"I think we played stupid," said Roy, who suddenly doesn't look so invincible, just as thug Claude Lemieux suddenly doesn't look so menacing. With 6:34 left, as players grappled, Lemieux refused to join the fray, skating with stick in hand, waving it at Vyacheslav Kozlov, the smallest player on the ice, instead of facing Rouse, who was prepared to fight.

It was an act of cowardice, which should surprise no one. This was supposed to be the game that tested the Wings' mettle. Roy had deemed it so, coyly wondering if the Wings were willing to "pay the price."

The same now is asked of the Avs.

"Obviously, we didn't respond," Crawford said. "And we're not proud of the way we performed. This is one where you lick your wounds and come back the next game."

The grisly finish was unfortunate but predictable between teams that harbor real, undiluted hate for each other. It clouded two periods of breathtaking hockey by the Wings. The Russian magicians accounted for four goals and reduced the brash Roy to humorous displays of distemper, lashing at officials, slashing at players. He wasn't around for the end, pulled after two periods, when Crawford waved the white hanky his team had already displayed.

We predicted the champs would not go quietly, but now we feel foolish, and so must they.

The Wings kept plugging, the Avs started mugging. It won't be long now. Whatever it takes: hits, goals, fighting back. The Wings are using it all. The Avs are losing it all.

AVALANCHE BEAT RED WINGS BY A LANDSLIDE

BY CYNTHIA LAMBERT

The Detroit News

THE RED WINGS wanted to give the Colorado Avalanche a fight on Saturday night. Instead, they gave them exactly what they didn't want to — life.

Colorado's 6-0 victory against the Wings in Game 5 of the Western Conference finals did more than give the Avalanche a chance to remain in the series. It gave the defending Stanley Cup champions proof that they still have it.

"It was tough here tonight," said Claude Lemieux, who scored Colorado's first two goals. "We were three to win, now we have two to go. I said before that we believed in ourselves. We believe again and we're going to keep believing."

Detroit leads the best-of-seven series three games to two. Game 6 is

Wings goalie Mike Vernon was removed after allowing Colorado's fourth goal.

Monday night at Joe Louis Arena. If the Avalanche win, Game 7 would be Thursday night in Denver.

The Avalanche were missing star center Peter Forsberg, who was out because of a leg injury. But the other stars showed the way, while the Red Wings played their worst game of the postseason.

"We deserved to be embarrassed with the way we played," Brendan Shanahan said. "It was almost appropriate we got shellacked. This was something we haven't done since Game 4 in St. Louis (a 4-0 loss). We were awful tonight. As a team, there wasn't one good thing to say about this game. There wasn't a single player who was happy with his play. Now we have to get back quickly."

Lemieux scored twice by 11:04 of th first. Valeri Kamensky had four assists, Joe Sakic scored twice and had one assist, and goalie Patrick Roy stopped the Wings early to deaden Stephane Yelle and Scott Young also scored for Colorado.

Roy posted his third shutout of the playoffs this year and 11th of his career.

Mike Vernon started in net for Detroit, but was replaced by Chris Osgood after Colorado's fourth goal.

"This kind of game by them was to be expected," Vernon said. "They had their backs to the wall. They were gung-ho for tonight. We knew this was going to be a long series and it's turning out to be a bit of a roller-coaster ride."

The Wings can only hope it doesn't turn into Demon Drop. But what happens is under their control. They likely have learned a lesson after com-

The Avalanche had plenty to celebrate during an easy victory over the Wings.

GAME 5

Red Wings

0

Avalanche

6

at Colorado
May 24, 1997

ing out flat against the Avalanche.

"We were playing the Stanley Cup champions and I think a lot of people had written them off," Steve Yzerman said.

"They rebounded after a 6-0 loss and we'll do that, too. We allowed them to do this. They were very assertive and we didn't respond to that."

Roy was strong from the start to prevent the Wings from taking an early lead. Detroit controlled the play for the first few minutes and took the first three shots.

The Avalanche began to find a way around the Wings' defense at about six minutes into the first. Detroit's defense was slower than in previous games and the forwards didn't help

because they could not carry the play.

At 6:46 of the first, Lemieux flipped a rebound high over Vernon, who was sitting on the ice after missing a chance to freeze a rebound. Lemieux thrust his left fist into the air after scoring.

The Wings missed a great chance at 9:30 to tie the score when Darren McCarty had a breakaway. He fired high on his first shot, and had two more tries from close range, but was stopped by Roy. In Game 2, McCarty scored high on Roy's glove side to seal a 4-2 victory.

"That's the way he scored on that (first) game," Roy said. "And that's why I gave it to him. He hit the top of my glove and it went over the top of the net."

Lemieux's first goal and Roy's saves on McCarty helped Colorado maintain momentum. At 11:04, Lemieux struck again, popping in a rebound of a Sandis Ozolinsh slap shot from the left point.

WINGS FLY INTO FINALS

By Cynthia Lambert
....
The Detroit News

Goodbye, Colorado Avalanche. Hello, Philadelphia Flyers.

The Red Wings bade farewell to the Avalanche on Monday night with a 3-1 victory at Joe Louis Arena to advance to the Stanley Cup Finals for the second time in three years.

The Wings clinched the Western Conference finals in six games, the same number Colorado needed last season to eliminate the Wings before winning the Cup. The Wings will open the Finals in Philadelphia on Saturday night.

GAME 6

Red Wings

3

Avalanche

1

at Detroit
May 26, 1997

"We talked about it (Sunday)," Wings Coach Scotty Bowman said. "If you're going to beat a champion, you can't outpoint them. You have to knock them out. We didn't want to go back to Colorado.

"When you can knock out a Stanley Cup winner with one game, you should do it. You don't want to, when you're my age, be looking back and say you didn't show up for the game. You'd never forgive yourself."

Sergei Fedorov must have been listening to Bowman. He showed up, and risked his body to stay in the game.

At 5:31 of the first period, Fedorov collided with defenseman Aaron Miller, causing Fedorov's elbow to jam into his side. His diaphragm went into spasms, he couldn't catch his breath and he had to leave the game.

Doctors told Bowman after the first period that Fedorov might be able to return for the third. But after being told by captain Steve Yzerman how important he was to the team, Fedorov returned midway through the second with the energy of a player taking his first shift in the season opener.

"I was excited to get back," Fedorov said. "When I got back to the bench, I let everyone know I was there. I started saying, 'Let's do it, let's do it.'"

Martin Lapointe sends a shot past Colorado goalie Patrick Roy as Claude Lemieux looks on.

At 6:11 of the third period, with the Wings leading 1-0, Fedorov did it. He took a pass from Vyacheslav Kozlov and sent a hard shot at Patrick Roy from close range. Roy made the save, but Fedorov scored on the rebound to make it 2-0.

"Sergei is an unbelievable talent," Kris Draper said. "When a player like him gets hurt, you want him back as soon as possible. When he came back, he sat next to me and asked how I felt. I told him I felt great. He said, 'Me too.' When one of your best players says that, that's all you want to hear. Then he comes out and gets the game-winning goal. It was a perfect script for him."

The Wings needed Fedorov's goal because Scott Young scored on a rebound of Adam Deadmarsh's shot at 14:48 of the third to make it 2-1. But the Wings persevered, as they had throughout the series.

Brendan Shanahan scored into an empty net with 29.8 seconds left to make it 3-1 and send the Wings to the Finals for the 20th time.

"It was such a relief to get that

empty-netter," Shanahan said. "Now it's back to work. The Stanley Cup still hasn't been won."

But the Wings will take something more to the Finals than memories of holding the Clarence Campbell bowl. They will take an improved, and wiser, team.

"I think we played better than them," Martin Lapointe said of the Avalanche. "It's nice to see they couldn't step up. We beat them on the boards, to the puck. We showed a lot of heart tonight."

The same could not be said of the Avalanche, who were outshot, 42-16. Roy was outstanding in keeping his team in the game.

"Patrick kept us in it and gave us a chance to steal one," Avalanche Coach Marc Crawford said. "But at this point in the year, you don't steal one. The whole group of us has to take a big, long look in the mirror and learn the lessons."

Said the Wings' Darren McCarty: "We had so many opportunities throughout the game to win it. Hats off to Patrick Roy. He played outstanding."

The Wings recovered from a 6-0 loss in Game 5 Saturday night in Denver. Not only did they want to end the series at home, they also desperately wanted to avoid returning to Denver, where the Avalanche were 8-1 in the postseason.

"I think that's a safe assumption," McCarty said. "When you have the opportunity to win a series at home, you've got to do it.

"This is really such a great feeling. But Joey (Kocur) said it all when we were huddled around after the game. He said, 'Don't worry, boys, the next one feels even better.'"

The next one would be the Stanley Cup, which has eluded the Red Wings since 1955 — the longest drought in the NHL.

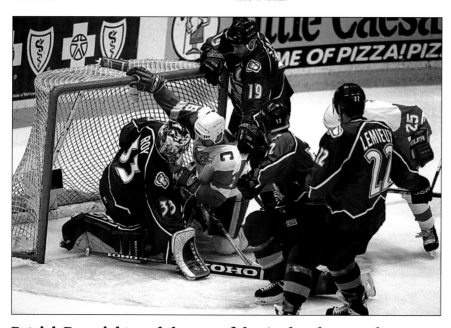

Patrick Roy, right, and the rest of the Avalanche went home instead of to the Stanley Cup Finals. There will be no repeat for the Avs.

They waited a year for this, but the true glory awaits

BY BOB WOJNOWSKI

The Detroit News

They waited a year for this night, for this moment. They plotted for it, sweated about it, stewed about it. With relentlessness and ruthlessness, the RedWings returned to get what they believed was theirs, and in 60 minutes of splendid hockey, they took it with force.

Passion burning and skates flying, stoked by all the emotions — revenge, desperation, anger — the Wings could not be stopped, not by a Hall of Fame goalie, not by the defending Stanley Cupchampions. Colorado has been vanquished, and so have the Wings'ghtmares of Claude Lemieux, swept away by Detroit's series-clinching 3-1 victory Monday night.

It ended with Brendan Shanahan firing the puck into an empty net with 29.8econds left, eliciting wave after wave ofear-splitting cheers, stored for a year, orlonger. The ugliest ghosts have been shooed, and now a Stanley Cup Final with Philadelphia awaits.

To truly feel the emotion, you had tosee the postgame handshakes, when the players lined up ... everyone but two. Kris Draper, mangled by Lemieux a year ago in Colorado's victory,did not shake Lemieux's hand. Darren McCarty, who extracted the first ounces of revenge two months ago, also didn't shake. Lemieux

turned his head and skated past, beaten the only way it really matters.

Then, as the crowd roared, Draper skated to the bench and hugged his teammates.

"It would have been nice if he'd had something to say," Draper said. "It was the sweetest win I've been involved in. It was a long grind, a long year. This is what we were working for."

At the end of this long grind, there was a short ride. Captain Steve Yzerman skated across the ice withthe Clarence Campbell bowl, signifying the Western Conference championship. He raised it once, salutedthe crowd, and was done, one more round to go.

"We've been through a lot the last couple of years," Yzerman said. "You realize after being in the Finals that finishing second means absolutely nothing."

"On to the big show," Mike Vernon said to the cameras, as cool and calm as he was all series.

The Wings went after this game like hounds on pork chops, chewing the Avalanche savagely. They outshot Colorado, 42-16, and if not for goalie Patrick Roy, would have settled matters with ease. They won the battles in the corners, in front of the nets, behind the benches.

Scotty Bowman has the Wings in the Finals for the second time in three years, delivered there on a current of

red passion. Detroit needed this one to forestall a Game 7 in Denver, to fell the champs before they got back up.

"I told the team they would rue the day if they didn't show up and play the game of their lives," Bowman said. "When you can knock out a Stanley Cup champion in one game, you've got to do it."

Uh, the Wings got the message.

"We wanted it really bad," said Sergei Fedorov, who scored the second goal. "We wanted it more than anything in our lives."

Detroit was the superior team, and it was evident immediately. The Wings nursed no hangover from their 6-0 loss in Game 5 on Saturday, dominating from the start. This is how it went most of the series, with the Wings swarming and shooting and hoping Roy came tumbling down. He is the sport's all-time money goalie, and if the Wings were to win, they would have to beat the best.

With every whistling missile, you could see their resolve grow, as did Roy's. This was a classic confrontation — the brash goalie who had openly questioned whether the Wings were "willing to pay the price," against a team that simply refused to stop shooting.

Yzerman truly was a captain of distinction, diving at shots, hustling for pucks. McCarty played as ifpossessed, and maybe he has been since

Sergei Fedorov, right, and the rest of the Detroit Red Wings celebrate a Game 6 victory over the Avalanche and a Western Conference title.

Avalanche Coach Marc Crawford said. "They wore us down. They didn't let us do anything we wanted."

Sometimes the wait heightens the taste, and the Wings have dreamed of this moment since May last year, when Lemieux shattered Draper's face and the Avalanche shattered the Wings. Everything the Wings did since — the trade for Shanahan, McCarty's vengeance on Lemieux, the quest to get bigger and tougher — was for this moment, Monday night, when their nightmare finally ended.

After Detroit beat Colorado on March 26, when Lemieux's blood stained the Joe Louis Arena ice, the Avalanche's Mike Keane had dug one more time, declaring the Wings "gutless and heartless" and issuing this: "We'd love to see them again in the playoffs."

Well, they saw, and were conquered. Lemieux, master of the self-protective turtle move, is gone and the gutty Wings move on, branding this series "The Turtle vs. The Heir."

"The only way to end all that was to beat them and bury them," Draper said, smiling. "A lot of people doubted and wondered how we'd react. And from the drop of the puck in Game 1, we came out and fought hard."

The Wings stormed one throne, the one they had to have, and now eye the biggest one, abdicated in this city a tortuous 42 years ago. The Flyers are next, and it won't be easy. But today, the Wings and their fans should savor the cheers that shook the Joe as the seconds ticked away, as Shanahan's shot found the net.

It took a year of stewing and two weeks of sweating but the Wings grabbed what they had to have. The only thing left is to get it all.

his friend, Draper, was injured by Lemieux. Shanahan rose as we expected, the man brought here specifically to help beat Colorado.

When the Wings finally broke through, it happened suddenly, innocently. At 3:29 of the second period, Martin Lapointe lifted a quick shot ... a bounce ... a flub ... a goal, trickling off Roy's arm.

The Wings never let up, as they rarely have this postseason. They haven't been outshot in 16 games, haven't lost at home in seven. Goalie

Vernon hardly was tested, but when he was, he rose. In the second period, Lemieux had a chance but his shot hit Vernon's stick, a goal if it goes an inch either way.

Yes, this was a game decided in the smallest margins, by the Wings' disciplined defense, which protected Vernon wonderfully. For all the shots, this is how the Wings win, by avoiding dumb penalties, by building a wall at the blue line and daring anyone to skate through.

"By far, they were the better team,"

Front row, left to right: Bob Goldham, Len Kelly, James Skinner (coach), Terry Sawchuk, Ted Lindsay, Marty Pavelich. Second row: Carl Mattson (trainer), Earl Reibel, Tony Leswick, Marcel Bonin, John Wilson, Bill Dineen, Lefty Wilson (assistant trainer). Third row: Vic Stasiuk, Marcel Pronovost, Jim Hay, Benny Woit, Glen Skov, Alex Delvecchio and Gordie Howe.

Times have changed since Cup's last visit

BY JOE FALLS

The Detroit News

IMAGINE THIS: DARREN MCCARTY AND CLAUDE LEMIEUX GOING INTO the same penalty box and sitting next to each other, separated only by a stadium guard. Or maybe an usher.

Mayhem.

They would have to paint the penalty box red to hide the blood.

But that's how it was in Olympia Stadium in 1955 — when the Red Wings won the Stanley Cup.

A lot of things were different 42 years ago. None of these modern-day Red Wings was even born, and Scotty Bowman was 22 years old and had not even thought about coaching. He was trying to think of ways to pay his grocery bill.

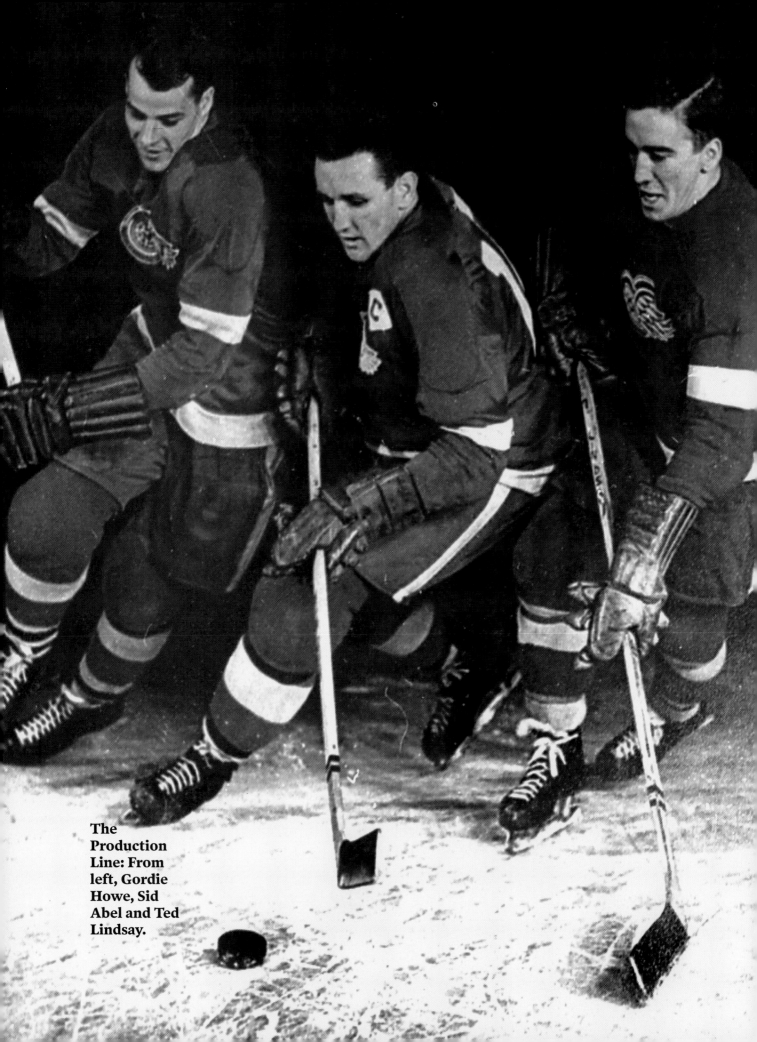

The Production Line: From left, Gordie Howe, Sid Abel and Ted Lindsay.

It was a simple time in many ways. World War II was over for 10 years and the country was at peace. We were in the middle of the Dwight D. Eisenhower presidency and the main thrust was to buy a home, buy a car and begin raising your children.

Some have called it one of the most tranquil periods in our history. Nothing much was going on except living quiet, peaceful lives.

Only a few of us had television sets. Drugs were something you got at the drug stores. Drive-in theaters were big, and frozen vegetables were starting to appear in markets.

The year 1955 was a time when: Jazz saxophonist Charley Parker died, Winston Churchill retired as Prime Minister of Great Britain, *Cat on a Hot Tin Roof* opened on Broadway, Bill Vukovich died trying for his third straight Indy 500 victory, former Argentina president Juan Peron was ousted, painter Grandma Moses turned 95, President Eisenhower had a heart attack, the Brooklyn Dodgers won their first World Series, 24-year-old actor James Dean died when his Porsche Spider crashed, the *Mickey Mouse Club and the Mouseketeers* debuted on TV, Cy Young died and *Damn Yankees* became the theater hit of the year.

We were just starting to pick up *Hockey Night in Canada* on Saturday nights (first, the weekly bath, then Foster Hewitt from the Gondola in Maple Leaf Gardens.) We were never sure what the Gondola was, but it hung high over The Gardens and it seemed like the most wonderful place in the world.

How could somebody be so lucky to work in a Gondola. It was Hewitt's broadcast booth and we got the same thrill every Saturday night when he began the show: "Hello, Canada. It is clear and cold in Toronto and we're talking to you from the Gondola high in Maple Leafs Gardens."

And, of course, it was Murray Westgate with that mechanic's cap, pleasant smile and neat, gray hair who sold us our gas and oil, just before those sports writers and broadcasters started in with their "Hot Stove League" between the periods. (I always thought they had a hot stove hidden somewhere in the studio, but I never did see it).

And then, what we all waited for: Hewitt's favorite call — "He shoots, he scores!" Maybe it wasn't as glamorous as Maple Leaf Gardens, but Olympia Stadium in Detroit wasn't bad.

They had Apps, Drillon, Broda, Kennedy, Ezinicki and Hewitt; we had Abel, Lindsay, Howe, Kelly, Delvecchio, Pronovost and Al Nagler. I always wished Nagler would stop calling Vic Stas-IUK, Vic Stas-IAK. But he never did.

How those penalty boxes remained standing was, in retrospect, rather amazing. We just didn't know any better. We didn't even have Zambonis in those days, just four guys pushing two tanks of water around the ice between periods to smooth things out. We always told ourselves it was hot water because hot water would freeze quicker than cold water. That didn't make any sense but that's what someone said and it was a nice thing to know. You'd tell one of your buddies that the water was hot — "Look at the way it steams" — and this gave you an edge on him because he didn't know one way or the other.

Hey, there were a lot of things we didn't know in 1955. We had never heard of Brigitte Bardot, Sputnik, slap shots, crack, Dealy Plaza, Ali, the Beatles, Watts, Johnny Carson, Martin Luther King, Chappaquiddick, Kent State, Saigon, *Jaws*, Beirut, *Taxi Driver*, HIV, "Make my day," Jonestown, "One small step for man ...," Margaret Thatcher, Mother Teresa, the Wall crumbles, Super Bowl, Blues Brothers, Chris Osgood, Ted Turner, Nelson Mandella, skud missiles, John Gotti, *Rain Man*, *Les Miz*, Chernobyl, CNN, Tiananmen Square, E-Mail.

Did I tell you about the night Mr. Lindsay met Mr. Bill Ezinicki in our penalty box?

Most of the times the guys behaved themselves in there. They learned to cool off and, besides, they didn't want the guards or ushers to get hurt. They didn't make much money and didn't need this kind of grief.

Lindsay and Ezinicki got into a stick duel on the ice and were sent off for two minutes. A lot of words and some pushing and shoving took place in the penalty box, with a few swings over the head and behind the back of the poor guy sitting between them.

When their penalties expired, they stepped on the ice and went right at each other. Ezinicki swung his stick and hit Lindsay on the shoulder. Lindsay swung his stick and missed. That was the last time he missed.

Lindsay started swinging his fists and landed about 10 straight blows. Ezinicki didn't get off so much as a punch. He finally fell face first to the ice, with Lindsay falling on him and pounding the back of his head. Ezinicki's blood started staining the ice.

The officials looked on almost indifferently, as if to say: "Well, it's just those two — let them go."

It was not a pleasant sight but that's how it went between these two men. A pair of ruffians, they hated each other. One wore the Blue and White of the Maple Leafs, the other the winged wheel of the Red Wings.

That was more than enough for a little mayhem. There weren't too many teams to hate in those days — just six.

The 1954-55 season was the first time teams began using backup goalies. If a goalie got hurt, well, the trainer or one of the other players would take over. A strange tactic that would not be allowed in today's big-money matches. But it was romantic at the time and no one ever questioned such strategy.

That season probably marked Gordie Howe's worst scoring slump in the NHL. He started fast with 20 goals in his first 37 games, but got just four over the next 17..

In November, Lindsay scored his 250th career goal. After playing five big seasons in the Detroit nets, Terry Sawchuk was replaced, without consultation, when General Manager Jack Adams and Coach Jimmy Skinner felt the strain of goaltending was affecting Sawchuk's work. Sawchuk was high-strung, often blowing up for no reason, and he brooded a lot when there didn't seem much to brood about.

Sawchuk was back after a few games and went on to win the Vezina Trophy as the league's No. 1 goalie.

On Jan. 22, Lindsay was given a 10-day suspension for striking a spectator with his stick in a game in Toronto. The incident occurred after Eric Nesterenko of the Leafs and Howe scuffled along the boards and the fan grabbed Howe's stick. As Howe pulled away, the fan reached over the boards to hit him. Lindsay, who was 30 or 40 feet away, rushed forward and struck the fan.

Actually, the fans were very calm in those days.

"When you played in Maple Leaf Gardens, it seemed like going to an opera," Lindsay said. "The people in the box red seats — now gold — were dressed like it was a formal affair. Suits, ties — even tuxedos. They made you feel you were undressed, even in your uniform.

"Anyone who acted up, like throwing something on the ice, was given a notice by the Maple Leafs' management. Even if they were season- ticket holders, some would have their tickets picked up."

In Detroit, there were no tuxedos. But the fans were well dressed — shirts, ties, jackets, with the women in some of their finest evening wear. The fans loved their hockey, even the violence, but always remained detached from the scene. They behaved themselves and did not try to become part of the show.

What was it like in Olympia Stadium?

The arena was located on Grand River and McGraw, just south of Grand Boulevard and next to Northwestern High School. It was about five miles from downtown Detroit.

Part of the excitement of going to a game was the traffic on Grand River. It was always horrendous, but a major part of the experience. You knew the jam-up would be there — more impossible than ever — and you tried to figure out small ways to get two cars ahead, or slip in front of the car next to you.

We all did it.

Once you could see the marquee blazing outside the arena (Tonight: Detroit vs. Boston), you could feel the adrenaline start running. You were getting close, but not that close. You would move 10 feet, then stop. Five feet, then stop.

What complicated matters is that the fans used to park in all kinds of places around Olympia Stadium — on the streets, in small lots, in alleys and even on front lawns, which were very small and could accommodate only a few cars. These would make the rest of the journey on foot, scrambling across Grand River by cutting between the cars, sometimes climbing over your hood if you were too close to the car in front, but again, you didn't mind. This was Hockey Night in Detroit.

The press lot was just beyond the traffic jam in front of Olympia Stadium and it was always with a sigh of relief when the guard waved you in to the right. You did it with much trepidation, though, because you knew the fans hurrying through the cold night air would start in on you when they saw the preferential treatment you were getting.

They would yell all kinds of things: "Big man! Big car! Big deal!"

"Hey, creep, pay your way!"

Or, if they recognized you: "Hey, Falls, good stuff lately. Who has been writing it for you?"

I used to wear a baseball cap and pull it down over my eyes. It didn't help.

The stadium, as I recall, seated a little more than 14,000. It had a balcony, which made it a real hockey rink, and the seats up high were only a couple of bucks.

The press box was just under the balcony and we were so close to the ice we could see Gordie Howe's eyes blinking from an injury he suffered

Gordie Howe, right, was more than just a goal scorer ... he could also throw some vicious checks.

when he collided with Ted Kennedy in the playoffs a few years earlier.

I worked for The Associated Press in those days and my seat was between Marshall Dann, the hockey writer for The Detroit Free Press, and Ross Jewell, the official scorer. Fred Huber, the Wings' erudite publicity man — he could do The New York Times crossword puzzle non-stop in ink — sat next to the official scorer.

Ross Jewell was a very nervous man. He even occasionally stuttered when he spoke. He would sit there,

almost terrified, watching the play. He didn't want to miss a play because a missed play meant criticism from somewhere. He was not up to criticism.

So he would follow the puck carefully and write down the numbers of the players as they touched the puck. If someone scored, he would simply back the numbers up two and give out the assists.

Even then, he was never sure of himself, and when a goal would go in quickly, or from a pileup, he would turn

around in panic and say: "What happened on that one?"

No replays, remember.

I never said anything. Neither did Dann. Huber, ever the intellect — there was nothing he didn't know — would ponder the question for a moment and say: "I can't be absolutely sure, but I think Gordie got the tip of his stick on the puck in the corner."

So, Howe was getting assists he didn't earn, or didn't need. A story like this today would be page-one headlines.

But then, this was 1955.

It was dangerous going into the Red Wings' dressing room. Sawchuk might be in one of his moods and any question could produce a tirade of profanity. All the other players were easy to talk to and they would kind of wink at you as you approached Sawchuk's locker.

In other words: "Not tonight. Stay away."

The room would be strewn with orange slices. Some of these the players ate. Some were thrown at them between periods by Adams. Jolly Jack had a way of getting his message across, by the way he would carry train tickets to Indianapolis in his vest pocket — the city where the Red Wings' farm club played — and they were there for all to see.

The Wings used to play exhibition games against Michigan in Ann Arbor and Michigan State in East Lansing as a way to promote hockey. One time,

Olympia Stadium was home to large crowds, winning hockey and a family atmosphere.

they nearly lost to Michigan. Adams was furious. The moment the team entered the dressing room, he began shouting at a player named Al Dewsbury.

"Nobody ever plays that way for the Detroit Red Wings!" Adams said. "Nobody ever embarrasses this team that way!"

He threw a train ticket at Dewsbury's feet and stormed out of the dressing room. The young man was never heard from again.

Olympia Stadium had a family-type atmosphere. The fans would come in early and stand in the back lobby and greet the players as they came in from the parking lot. Fathers. Mothers. Grandfathers. Grandmothers. And children..

No one asked for autographs. Maybe a few children did, but it was never much of a deal. They all grew to know each other on a first-name basis.

It was the same after the games. The fans would gather in the back lobby to say goodnight to the players, and what was noticable is that players never left quickly, even though their own families might be waiting for them.

They were happy to hang around and chat with the fans. Then, it was on to Chuck Joseph's restaurant on Grand River for a steak and a few beers. Oddly enough, the fans did not follow them there. They knew their place. They were glad to spend some time with the players at the stadium; now it was time to leave them alone.

Another dangerous thing about going into the Red Wings dressing room in those days was trying to interview Howe. He was usually the story of the night and so you had to interview him most of the time.

Be careful, my friend.

He did not like talking about himself.

You would walk up to his locker and he would lean on you with those massive shoulders and pin you against the wall. It hurt, but not so much you couldn't stand it. He had learned how to apply the right pressure for each writer who came around.

You are not about to say much when you are fighting for your breath.

I always wore my overcoat into the dressing room, hoping to absorb some of the pain, but it never really worked.

"Get off me, you big oaf. When are you going to grow up?"

Howe would smile at you. No, make that a leer. He was great at leering.

Once he let you off the wall, he would throw an elbow into your ribs. You knew it was coming but could do nothing about it. He did it so quickly, again administering a dose of pain but nothing you couldn't stand.

Then — and I'll never know how he learned to be so adept — he would reach out and grab the tip of your privates through your pants and give it a little squeeze. That was it — the sign that there would be no interview on this evening. So, you would walk across the room, trying to keep your dignity, in search of someone less provocative, less physical, like maybe Red Kelly, who would almost blush anytime you tried to interview him.

No. 9, of course, was grinning by now. Another one in the victory column.

It was easy interviewing Lindsay. He always had something to say — and he always had the look of an imp in his eye, as if he had just stolen something, but you would never know what it was. You were never sure if you were getting the straight dope from Lindsay,

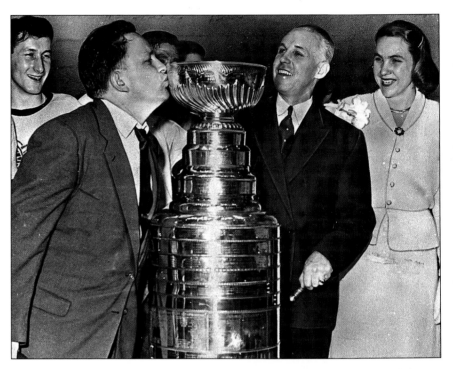

Bill Dineen, Coach Jimmy Skinner (kissing Cup), NHL president Clarence Campbell and Marge Norris celebrate the 1955 title.

but with those scars all over his face, you knew he had earned the right to tell you whatever he wanted. Besides, that crooked smile always took you in. They were really terrific guys in those days — great players and great gentlemen.

Detroit met Toronto in the semifinals in 1955 and won in four straight. The Leafs were without Tim Horton, their great defenseman, and they didn't have much of a power play and the Wings had no trouble handling them.

The Wings and Canadiens went seven games in the finals — rough, fast and without any overtimes. The Wings were in the closing stages of winning seven straight league titles and four Stanley Cups in seven years. Montreal was about to embark on its great run of five straight Stanley Cups with a team many still call the best ever.

Montreal lost the first two games in Olympia Stadium but won the next two in the Montreal Forum. It was in this series that the Canadiens ended a 15-game winning streak by Detroit.

With two goals in the final game, Alex Delvecchio was the hero in the Wings' Cup-clinching victory.

And what was the reaction in Detroit?

Not much.

Everyone had grown accustomed to the Red Wings winning, so it was no big deal. In The Detroit News the next day, the story got third play on the sports page.

It was the opening day of the baseball season and the Tigers dominated the sports pages. The hockey story, written by Harry Stapler, barely made it above the fold of the sports section front. A baseball picture was played over the hockey picture. And there was just one other hockey story, buried inside the section.

Bill Cusimano, the man who threw the first octopus a few years earlier, remembers the night the Red Wings won it all in 1955. He was a friend of Delvecchio and asked if he could have his stick when the game was over.

When it ended, Delvecchio skated to the sideboards and tried to hand his stick to Cusimano. Several fans grabbed for it. Delvecchio pulled it back and finally worked it to his friend.

"I had a treasure and didn't know it," Cusimano said. "I had the stick which scored two goals and won the Stanley Cup. So what did I do with it. I used it in our Belle Isle games on Sunday and when we used to rent the Windsor Arena for 40 bucks an hour at five o'clock in the morning. I busted it.

"Just think what that stick would be worth today. Not in money but in history. I hope Alex never reads this book."

Adams was a man who liked to party. If the Red Wings were in Boston, he thought nothing of taking the entire press delegation to dinner at LockObers — one of the fine eating establishments on the East Coast.

When the Red Wings won Cups in 1954 and 1955, he invited the press (which was comprised mostly of writers) to a party at Yeaman, s nightclub on Howard Street in downtown Detroit. My wife and I drank from the Stanley Cup and danced until dawn.

She was thrilled with my new job.

"How often do they have these parties?" she said.

And I said: "Every year, my dear. Every year."

Gordie Howe celebrates his second goal during the Wings' 3-1 victory in the clinching game of the 1955 Stanley Cup Finals.

THE FINALS

Joe Kocur, part of the Red Wings' Grind Line, beats Ron Hextall in the first period.

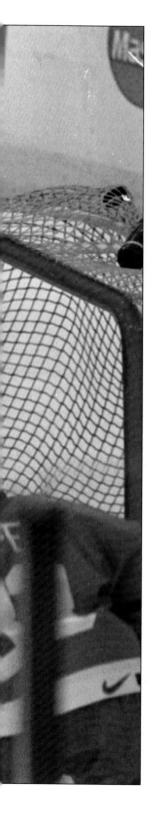

WINGS SOLVE HEX

First Finals win since 1966

BY CYNTHIA LAMBERT

The Detroit News

THE RED WINGS CHASED ONE MORE GHOST from their past on Saturday night, when they defeated the Philadelphia Flyers, 4-2, in Game 1 of the Stanley Cup Finals.

The Detroit franchise won for the first in the Finals since it defeated the Montreal Canadiens on April 26, 1966. That victory gave the Wings a 2-0 series lead, but they ended up losing in six games.

"It's great to win one game," associate coach Dave Lewis said. "Nobody talked about it much, but ... this means a lot to the guys."

GAME 1

Red Wings

4

Flyers

2

at Philly
May 31, 1997

Kris Draper and the Red Wings struck early against the stunned Flyers in Game 1.

The last time the Wings made it this far, they were chased away in four straight by the New Jersey Devils. Since then, the Wings have been waiting to avenge the disgrace. Saturday's victory gave them a start.

"I think it's a huge pat on the back for us," said Mike Vernon, who turned aside 26 shots. "In our series vs. New Jersey, we were very disappointed and embarrassed by what happened. I can look back now and see that we were beat in every area of the game, not just in goals, but in shots and everything. But we learned a valuable lesson from the Devils, and we bring that into this series."

Of course, after a poor showing in Game 1, the Flyers also have motivation from a negative experience.

"We didn't skate well, we didn't support the puck well," captain Eric Lindros said. "We knew what they were going to do, and we didn't do what we had to do to counter that."

Instead, the Flyers tried to rely heavily on their size, a plan for which the Wings prepared.

"They're a physical hockey club," Kris Draper said. "I don't know if we outsmarted them as much as outskated them. I know that's something that I have to do, since most of their guys have 40 or 50 pounds on me. That's my asset."

But scouting also was a Wings asset. Entering the series, they knew the Flyers were vulnerable to defensive lapses. The Wings took advantage of many of those, and exposed Ron Hextall as a goalie they could easily beat — at least on this night.

Hextall gave up first-period goals to Kirk Maltby — the culmination of a two-on-none with Kris Draper — and Joe Kocur, and a second-period goal on a long wrist shot by Sergei

The Flyers' Petr Svoboda (23) and the Wings' Darren McCarty (25) clash during the first period.

Fedorov. But his biggest mistake came on Steve Yzerman's slap shot from the blue line 56 seconds into the third.

The timing of Yzerman's goal was crucial, since it came so quickly into the final period, when the Flyers had to come out strong.

Vernon preserved the Wings' lead late in the third when he made his best save of the game, on Trent Klatt at 14:22. Klatt, at the right circle, took a pass from Lindros and fired a shot at Vernon. He came out of the net to cut the angle.

"What made that save easier is that Vladimir (Konstantinov) and Stevie (Yzerman) came back to take the pass back away," Vernon said. "I thought Klatt might try to go back to Lindros, but they covered that. I came out and got my glove on the puck."

Rod Brind'Amour (power play) and John LeClair scored for the Flyers. Brind'Amour's came in the first period, and at first it appeared as if Yzerman had scored inadvertently. But Yzerman said Brind'Amour had extended his stick to tap the puck past Vernon during a flurry in front of the net.

LeClair scored late in the second to trim the Wings' lead to 3-2 entering the third. But Yzerman's goal distanced the Flyers again.

The Flyers were never able to try to pull Hextall from the net for the extra attacker. Lindros took a frustration penalty at 17:48 when he slugged Konstantinov in the face, basically sending the Wings on the power play for the rest of the game.

Flyers goalie Ron Hextall was left frazzled after Game I.

Wings unafraid of Flyers

BY BOB WOJNOWSKI
....
The Detroit News

So, who's afraid of the big, nasty Flyers? If that was the first question of the Stanley Cup Finals — and really, it was — the Red Wings provided the first definitive answer: Not us.

Not the Wings' bashing Grind Line, which added offense to its chores. Not goalie Mike Vernon, who stood up as the Flyers crowded his crease and stormed his net. This was billed as Philadelphia's hulking Legion of Doom, led by Eric Lindros, against the Wings' speedy Masters of Vroom. The Flyers tried to rile the Wings, to knock them off thepuck and off their game, but they wouldn't fluster.

So chalk up Detroit's 4-2 victory in Game One Saturday night to poise and punch, for maintaining the former and avoiding the latter. The Wings have proven they're capable of playing any foe, any style. The Flyers and their frazzled goalie, Ron Hextall, just got their first lesson.

"We're going to do what we can, take the hits and give as many as we

Game One: Where the Wings shot from

● Goal   ● Shot

The Red Wings outshot the Flyers, 30-28, but both teams had plenty of good scoring opportunities. Here is a breakdown of the Wings' individual shots:

No.	Player	Shots
2	Slava Fetisov	1
5	Nicklas Lidstrom	4
13	Vyacheslav Kozlov	1
14	Brendan Shanahan	4
16	Vladimir Konstantinov	1
17	Doug Brown	1
18	Kirk Maltby	2
19	Steve Yzerman	3
20	Martin Lapointe	1
25	Darren McCarty	1
26	Joe Kocur	3
28	Tomas Sandstrom	1
55	Larry Murphy	2
91	Sergei Fedorov	5

Period 1

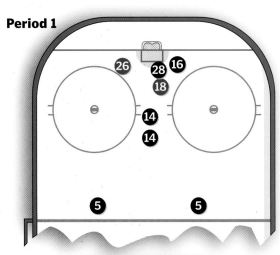

Period 2

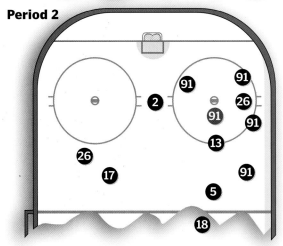

Period 3

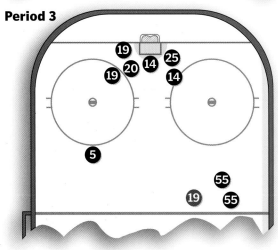

can," said Joey Kocur, who scored his first goal of the playoffs. "Our game plan is to get on them as quickly as possible and slow them down, and that's what we did."

While the Flyers played sloppily and even a bit timid, the Wings again showed the maturity they used to lack. This was a game of mistakes — Philadelphia's weak defense made the most miscues, Hextall made the most glaring. Just when the Flyers seemed capable of turning dangerous, captain Steve Yzerman whistled a slapshot from the blue line 56 seconds into the third period, beating a befuddled Hextall cleanly for the goal that sealed the victory.

The Flyers' final act of frustration came with 2:12 left, when Lindros speared and slugged Vladimir Konstantinov, drawing a penalty that effectively killed any comeback.

It was the Grind Line of Kocur, Kirk Maltby and Kris Draper that set the tone. They opened the game against Lindros' line and didn't back off, not for a single shift. Kocur, who was playing in a 30-and-over beer league in December before convincing the Wings he still had NHL value, tried a different shot and chaser this time. He stole an errant pass by Kjell Samuelsson and beat Hextall with a fancy backhander late in the first period, providing a 2-1 lead the Wings never relinquished.

Earlier, Maltby and Draper had netted the first goal on a pretty passing play that ended with Maltby firing the puck over Hextall's shoulder. Now, if you're the Flyers, this is what you're thinking: Kocur? ... Maltby? ... Uh-oh.

"That was important, it gave us a chance to take the pressure off the big guys," Draper said. "We get those two guys scoring and it incites the team."

Really, this is the hidden strength of the Wings, their ability to attack with four lines, four different ways. Sergei Fedorov scored the third goal on a two-on-one, surprising Hextall with a quick slapper. It was the outside game (Fedorov and Yzerman) and the inside game (Kocur, Maltby, Draper), and the Flyers were too busy trying to hit somebody to know what hit them.

The Wings had waited two years to redeem their humbling sweep at the hands of New Jersey in the 1995 finals, and they arrived Saturday night looking like they'd spent their time wisely, building confidence, practicing poise.

They also seemed to skate more freely, and maybe it's because they aren't lugging the old favorite's role.

The Wings are underdogs — "HUGE underdogs" Scotty Bowman said earlier, with a smirk — and frankly, they don't mind. Every writer in both Philadelphia newspapers picked the Flyers to win the series, even after the Wings had vanquished defending champion Colorado with relative ease. There even were TV reports of parade preparations.

"That's the difference between this year and previous years," Maltby said. "There isn't the same pressure on us. It makes it easier to perform."

These Wings look like a team that has traveled this path before. They used to grip their sticks so

Mike Vernon continued his strong playoff play in Game 1.

tightly, they got splinters. But Yzerman keeps spouting the mantra — "Relax" — and Philadelphia could have used the advice.

The Flyers played skittish, while trying desperately to establish the physical game they brag about. They went hunting for big hits while the Wings went hunting for turnovers, and found their prize more often. The Flyers crashed the net with impunity, planting

Lindros in front of Vernon and daring anyone to move him.

But the Wings won because the Flyers turned it over repeatedly, and Detroit's role guys were able to capitalize. When the Grind Line scored twice, the message was clear: The Flyers will be punished for mistakes.

So they were, again and again. Three more games like this and the Wings will have answered everything.

WINGS' CUP HALF FULL

Shanahan Puts Philadelphia in Double Trouble

BY CYNTHIA LAMBERT

The Detroit News

THE RED WINGS PLAYED THEIR WAY into superb position Tuesday night, defeating the Philadelphia Flyers, 4-2, at the CoreStates Center to take a two-games-to-none lead in the best-of-seven Stanley Cup Finals.

The Wings return to Joe Louis Arena for games 3 and 4 on Thursday and Saturday with the odds of winning the series in their favor. Only three times since 1939 have teams rallied from a 2-0 deficit to win a Finals series, and only twice has a team lost the first two at home and won the series.

"We know the position we're in," defenseman Bob Rouse said. "We realize now we're that much closer and that we've put ourselves in a good position. But there's a lot of fight left

Garth Snow and the Flyers are looking up at Brendan Shanahan, left, and Martin Lapointe after Game 2.

GAME 2

Red Wings   Flyers

4   **2**

at Philly June 3, 1997

Skating off home ice trailing two games to none was not the way Flyers captain Eric Lindros, above, envisioned things.

in the Flyers and we know that, too."

The Wings also know what the Flyers are up against. In 1995, the Wings lost the first two games at home to the New Jersey Devils in the Finals, and were swept.

"The hunger level for us elevates now," said Brendan Shanahan, who scored twice. "We know winning on the road doesn't mean anything unless you can do it at home, too. There's a lot of hockey left in front of us yet."

Not if Philadelphia can't find better goaltending.

As in Game 1, soft goals allowed by the Flyers helped the Wings win. In Game 2, Garth Snow — not Ron Hextall — was the culprit.

"We have to have a higher responsibility to ... play better and it starts with the goaltender," Flyers coach Terry Murray said. "We had too many breakdowns and too many turnovers. That, and not getting big stops, are the biggest nightmare for a team in the Stanley Cup Finals."

Goaltending also was the story for the Wings. Mike Vernon was outstanding, making big saves throughout.

"I don't know what the perception is out there," Wings defenseman Larry Murphy said. "But anybody in this room definitely hasn't overlooked Mike and what he's done for us. The guys in here are thankful for him being there. In the room after the first two games,

everyone's come in and gone over and patted Mike on the back because we know what he's done for us."

Coach Scotty Bowman said Vernon was a key against the Flyers.

"He's an experienced goalie and the Flyers get a lot of people in front because of their size," Bowman said. "So for him it's a case of knowing when to cover the bottom of the net or when to freeze the puck. He's handling the puck very well in this series, and that has helped our defensemen because I thought tonight their shootins were better than they were in the first game."

Vernon, who is 14-4 in the playoffs this year, said he is playing the game he has always played.

"I'm just trying to get myself in good position," he said. "I'm not the type of goaltender to come way out of the net. I'm just trying to hold my ground."

Steve Yzerman had a power-play goal and Kirk Maltby also scored for the Wings. Shanahan's first goal and Maltby's were on shots from beyond the top of the faceoff circles.

Detroit led, 3-2, after two periods, and made it 4-2 thanks to a breakdown in the Philadelphia defense. The Wings got a two-on-one break, with Paul Coffey as the only Flyer back. Martin Lapointe, closing on the right, passed to Shanahan, whose shot from the left dot beat Snow.

Rod Brind'Amour scored two power-play goals on high deflections. But the goals weren't enough to offset a poor performance by Snow, who started after Hextall's subpar performance in Game 1.

"It seems like we're always chasing from behind," Flyers forward Mikael Renberg said. "That's a tough way to play."

Had the Flyers received better goaltending from Snow, the outcome might have been different. Unlike Game 1, the Flyers used their speed and were successful at dumping the puck in the Wings' zone and keeping it there with strong forechecking.

The Flyers' speed was boosted by lineup changes, and they tied the score despite the Wings taking a 2-0 lead by 9:22 of the first period.

"They did a few adjustments in the first half of the game," Bowman said. "I thought they made shorter passes. They had more speed through the neutral zone and we got trapped a few times. But I think we adjusted. We did

Game 2: Where the Wings shot from

Period 1

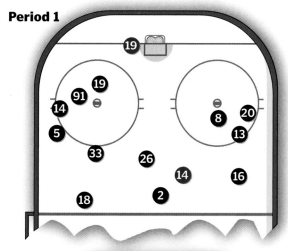

Period 2

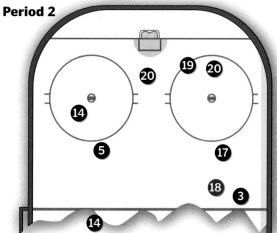

Period 3

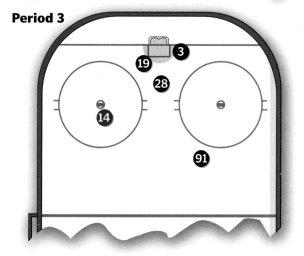

⬤ Goal ⬤ Shot

For the second time in the playoffs, the Wings were outshot by their opponent.

No.	Player	Shots
2	Slava Fetisov	1
3	Bob Rouse	2
5	Nicklas Lidstrom	2
8	Igor Larionov	1
13	Vyacheslav Kozlov	1
14	Brendan Shanahan	5
16	Vladimir Konstantinov	1
17	Doug Brown	1
18	Kirk Maltby	2
19	Steve Yzerman	4
20	Martin Lapointe	3
26	Joe Kocur	1
28	Tomas Sandstrom	1
33	Kris Draper	1
91	Sergei Fedorov	2

Shanny time

Brendan Shanahan answered the call and became the latest Wings hero with two goals in Game 2. The second goal gave the Wings a 4-2 lead at 9:56 of the third period. Here is how it happened:

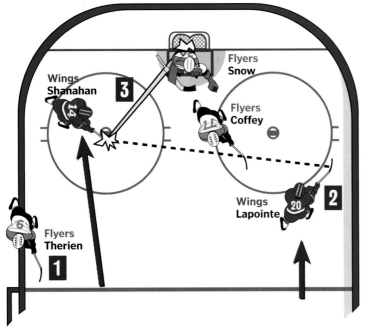

1 When defenseman Chris Therien (6) headed to the bench, the Wings caught the Flyers on a line change. Sergei Fedorov's quick pass from just inside the Wings' blue line got the play going.

2 Martin Lapointe (20) took Fedorov's pass at the red line and on the right wing, where he found himself on a two-on-one break with left wing Brendan Shanahan (14).

3 With only Paul Coffey (77) to beat, Lapointe, from the top of the right circle, fired a pass to Shanahan at the middle of the left circle. Shanahan one-timed a wrist shot past sprawling goalie Garth Snow (30).

---

adjust in the third period pretty well."

One of the Wings' best adjustments was something they have worked on throughout the playoffs. Even when the Flyers pressed, the Wings withstood the pressure because of tight checking and strong goaltending.

"I think we were able to remain composed throughout the game," Yzerman said. "Our goaltender made some real good saves. Our defensemen, I thought, were real solid in front of the net in blocking some shots and clearing pucks out. I don't think that we controlled the game by any means, but we were able to remain relatively composed when the heat got on us."

The Wings return to Detroit with a chance to take a commanding series lead Thursday night. Although his team is in dire straits, Flyers captain Eric Lindros placed the pressure on the Wings.

"We haven't had a lead to work with yet," Lindros said. "But the pressure is on them with a 2-0 lead. They are supposed to win it. We'll go to Detroit and see what happens."

FORGOTTEN MEN LEAD 'UNNORMAL' WINGS TO FINALS

BY BOB WOJNOWSKI

The Detroit News

Larry Murphy wasn't supposed to be here. He was supposed to be on a golf course by now, the boos of Toronto fans rattling in his head.

Mike Vernon wasn't supposed to be here. He was supposed to be traded, or benched, or otherwise forgotten.

Joe Kocur wasn't supposed to be here. He was supposed to be in a rec league, relishing retirement.

Tomas Sandstrom wasn't supposed to be here.

He was supposed to be enjoying the off-season in Pittsburgh, contemplating his pending free agency.

Doug Brown wasn't supposed to be here. He was supposed to be too small, no longer in Scotty Bowman's plans, trade bait.

Aaron Ward wasn't supposed to be here. He was supposed to be on the bench, a rookie watching the playoffs.

But they're here, in the Stanley Cup Finals, and they're a big rea-

The Flyers' Paul Coffey (white helmet) and the Wings' Kirk Maltby (18) clash at the boards during the third period.

his experience, and the defenseman has been dependable and occasionally dangerous. He had two assists in the Wings' 4-2 victory in Game 1.

"To get this far, it takes contributions from everyone," said Murphy, who won two Stanley Cups with Pittsburgh. "It's been that way throughout the history of the league."

Of course, you need help from all quarters. But these Wings are unique in their depth and versatility. They use four lines regularly and no one is dominating their scoring chart. Vernon has been excellent in goal, but the Wings aren't winning with one guy, or even a couple of guys, as teams generally do.

The last five Stanley Cup champions have been dominated by stars — Colorado (Joe Sakic, Patrick Roy), New Jersey (Claude Lemieux, Martin Brodeur), the Rangers (Mark Messier, Brian Leetch, Mike Richter), Montreal (Roy), Pittsburgh (Mario Lemieux).

For the Wings, the load has been spread from Sergei Fedorov to Slava Kozlov to Brendan Shanahan to Steve Yzerman to Igor Larionov to Vernon to ... Kocur.

Kocur, signed in December, scored on a breakaway in Game 1 and has been a physical presence throughout the playoffs. He was with the Rangers when they won in 1994 and he likes the look of this team.

"Teams that win do get those unnormal guys scoring," Kocur said. "It's an omen, or maybe it's just luck. You need luck. You need whatever it takes."

Whatever works. The Wings are dipping into all resources, tapping all sources. It might be unnormal, but it's working.

son the Red Wings are here. To win a Cup, it doesn't quite take a village, but it does take vigilance and persistence, and the Wings have at least half a dozen examples of it.

"When you get the opportunity, you try to make a difference," said Brown, who didn't play in 18 of the Wings' final 31 games, sat out the entire St. Louis series, then scored three goals against Anaheim. "We don't put the weight on one or two guys to carry us. It's important to persevere. Who knows where we'd be if guys went the other way?"

This is where Bowman's peculiar style pays dividends. Sure, he benches players without explanation, annoys them, riles them. But he doesn't bury them. After Vernon played poorly (as did the rest of the Wings) in the Finals against New Jersey two years ago, then had a protracted contract squabble, many assumed he was gone. Bowman wanted him back for times such as these, when you need a veteran.

Sandstrom, acquired from Pittsburgh for Greg Johnson, has provided muscle and smarts. Ward, who didn't play much at midseason, has become a physical force on the blue line.

Murphy looked slow and soft when he arrived from Toronto at the trading deadline. But Bowman liked

Yzerman, Shanahan help light the way

By John U. Bacon

The Detroit News

Probably no Red Wings had more pressure on them entering the playoffs than Steve Yzerman and Brendan Shanahan.

The Detroit fans and front office were waiting for Yzerman, the heart and soul of the Wings for almost a decade, to finally lead the team to a Stanley Cup. They expected Shanahan, the Wings' leading scorer, to be the long-missing piece to their playoff puzzle.

Through the first three series, Yzerman all but willed his team to victory in some games, but was virtually

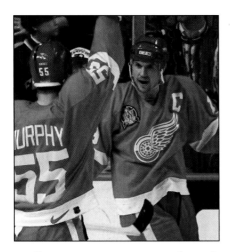

Defenseman Larry Murphy celebrates center Steve Yzerman's first-period power-play goal during the Wings' 4-2 victory.

invisible in others. Entering the Finals, his plus-minus rating stood at zero, and he hadn't had a point in five games.

Yzerman scored the final goal of the Red Wings' 4-2 victory in the first game of the Finals, then kept it going Tuesday night, beating Garth Snow on a scramble in front of the net. He also saved a goal in the second by tying up Rod Brind'Amour as a pass came through the slot.

After the game, Yzerman said the Wings' fruitless playoff runs the last two years have given them extra poise this time around. "We just feel a lot more comfortable," he said.

One reason is Shanahan, whom the Red Wings signed mainly to make them tougher in May and June. Shanahan did just that in the Wings' first 10 playoff games, getting four assists and three goals, two of them winners.

But before Tuesday night, Shanahan's points-per-game average had fallen steadily from 1.0 in the first series to .75 in the second to .67 in the third, against Colorado. Those aren't bad numbers, especially in the playoffs, but the trend wasn't promising with the most important games ahead.

Worse, in the five games preceding Game 2, Shanahan had two points: an assist in the 6-0 drubbing of Colorado in Game 4 and an open-net goal in Game 6.

So Shanahan's goal 1:37 into the first

period against Philadelphia on Tuesday provided a reassuring sign that he really was the clutch performer the Wings had hoped for when they traded for him.

Ironically, Shanahan's shot ricocheted off the foot of defenseman Paul Coffey, the trade bait the Wings used to get Shanahan. Coffey has been on the ice for six of the Wings' eight goals and in the penalty box for another.

Shanahan had a chance to put the Flyers away when he broke in alone on Snow in the second period. Snow dived at Shanahan, but Shanahan outwitted him by faking left and cutting right. Only a bouncing puck kept Shanahan from putting it away — and with it, possibly the game and the series.

"I guess I had about half a foot to shoot at, (but) I was trying to settle the puck down," Shanahan said.

The puck was nice and flat when Martin Lapointe fed Shanahan from the top of the right circle midway through the third period.

"Marty scored a lot of important goals from there, so the goalie has to challenge him," Shanahan said.

That explains why the net was so wide open for Shanahan when he redirected Lapointe's pass into it for the Wings' fourth goal.

After the game, Shanahan admitted he felt a lot of pressure since arriving in Detroit, but "it's better than not facing any pressure."

"Certainly it's a lot more fun when you're successful with it," he said.

Brendan Shanahan (14) is congratulated after scoring the Wings' first goal at 1:37 of the first period.

The Wings were in a mood to celebrate after Martin Lapointe's first-period goal.

ONE WIN AWAY

GAME 3
Red Wings | Flyers
6 | **1**
at Detroit June 5, 1997

Victory puts Wings close to Stanley Cup

BY BOB WOJNOWSKI

The Detroit News

THIS ISN'T ABOUT PHILADELPHIA NOW, not that it ever was. The Flyers are still out there simply because the NHL requires an opponent, to make it official.

The Red Wings are skating alone now, chasing something only they and their fans can truly see and understand. This is how a 42-year wait ends, with a pursuit so dogged, so dominating, it hardly matters who's on the other side.

Three periods of formality Saturday night are all that stand between the Wings and a sweep to the Stanley Cup, a distance reduced to the slimmest margin because the Wings will not let up, not for one second or one shift. They belted the Flyers 6-1 Thursday night to seize a 3-0 lead in the Finals, and they did it as they've done it all playoffs, with a disciplined defense, with help from every area, led by the captain, who has scored in all three games.

Steve Yzerman bagged the first goal, Sergei Fedorov and Martin Lapointe had two apiece and by the end, the fans were feasting, famished by the wait. As the lead mounted, they cheered huge hits by Vladimir Konstantinov, an assist by Mike Vernon on the sixth goal and a circus shot by Brendan Shanahan, who scored from behind the net, flipping the puck off beleaguered goalie Ron Hextall.

Obviously, the Flyers have no one to stop the puck, no one to stop the relentless Red Tide. There are too many Wings with too much to prove and it starts with Yzerman, who has waited 14 years for that skate around the rink. It's close now, so close, the ever-intense captain almost flashed a smile.

"It's exciting, it's a lot of fun, but it's also nerve-wracking," said Yzerman, greeted by a prolonged ovation from fans longing to celebrate. "Things have gone pretty well but you can't afford to relax."

The Wings will get hockey's highest prize because they're loaded with players talented and poised, driven by all the emotions — revenge, redemption, respect.

Fedorov? It was said he was too laid-back, didn't care enough about

Steve Yzerman's goal ignited the Red Wings' outburst in Game 3.

the Cup. It was a rap ridiculously leveled on Russian players, and Fedorov, with three goals in the series and eight in the playoffs, has refuted plenty with perhaps the best all-around

hockey of his career.

Vernon? The general in net just will not blink at the huge Flyers. A fan held up a sign for the once-maligned goalie that read simply, "Vernon — I apologize." With the victory, Vernon all but clinched another year on his contract and sealed his standing in Wings lore.

Shanahan? He has scored big goals, has led with emotion and elbows, and in this series, he has matched Philly's overrated toughness.

Scotty Bowman? He came here four seasons ago, suffered three humbling losses in the playoffs, adapted and retooled his team and is poised to deliver the goods.

Of course, before Bowman and his players accept any praise, they do have that little formality.

"We're three-fourths of the way there, that's the way I look at it," Bowman said. "I told the players to enjoy the win for five minutes, then start thinking about the next game."

This was the danger game for the Wings because a Philadelphia victory could have turned the series. But the Wings and their fans aren't squandering any more time. As the Flyers were introduced before the game, the fans drowned out P.A. announcer Bud Lynch with chants of "Let's Go Red Wings!"

The Wings have no discernible nerves now and nothing to fear, not even Eric Lindros. The Big Red Machine is revved and the only thing that can slow it is overconfidence or a sudden spate of misfortune.

"We've been good all year at learning from past disappointments and turning them into positives," Darren McCarty said. "We were up 3-1 and lost to Colorado, so we're going to get ready for the game of our lives."

Really, this is about persistence and patience now, which seem like different qualities, but not for the Wings. They're patient enough to wait for their chances and their

GameThree: Where the Wings shot from

Period 1

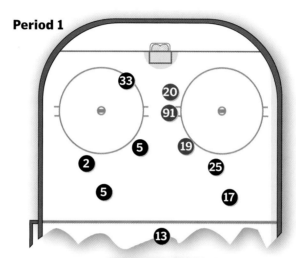

● Goal　　● Shot

Once again the Red Wings outshot their opponent, using puck movement and a stifling defense.

Period 2

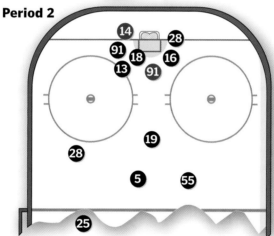

Period 3

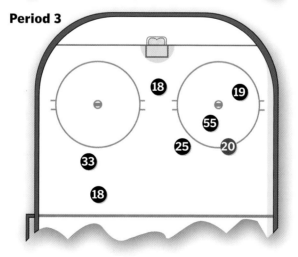

No.	Player	Shots
2	Slava Fetisov	1
5	Nicklas Lidstrom	3
14	Vyacheslav Kozlov	2
18	Brendan Shanahan	1
19	Vladimir Konstantinov	1
20	Doug Brown	1
25	Kirk Maltby	3
26	Steve Yzerman	3
28	Martin Lapointe	2
25	Darren McCarty	3
28	Tomas Sandstrom	2
33	Kris Draper	2
55	Larry Murphy	2
91	Sergei Fedorov	3

moment, persistent enough to create those chances, to demand that moment.

Even when Philadelphia grabbed a 1-0 lead, the Wings forced the play and didn't give the Flyers a chance to settle into a defensive shell. Not that it's possible to form a defensive shell when you've got a cracked shell in net. Hextall seems like a nice enough guy, but when he stops a puck these days, it's an accident.

You got the feeling early the only way the Wings could lose was if they gave it away. And in a shaky first period, they gave the Flyers four power plays, including a two-man advantage for 1:20. The Wings held firm, largely due to Yzerman's diligent penalty-killing, and when the Flyers failed, the wind and the will left them. The Wings — patiently, persistently — began to hammer.

It keeps coming back to the captain, exactly how it should be. He brought the franchise this far, he might as well push it the rest of the way. Two minutes after John LeClair provided the Flyers' first lead of the series, Yzerman took a quick pass from Vyacheslav Kozlov and fired it through the yawning gap between Hextall's legs.

Barely two minutes later, another Flyer giveaway led to another Detroit breakaway. We understand Philadelphia is the City of Brotherly Love, but really, the outpouring of compassion is startling. Karl Dykhuis lost the puck, Fedorov scooped it up and took a few strides before flipping a wrister past Hextall for a 2-1 lead.

Philly's weak two-man advantage followed and the Wings proceeded to take the game as if it was the clincher, swarming and smothering the Flyers. Lapointe, Mr. Feisty, grabbed the puck

Lapointe's big point

With the Red Wings ahead 2-1, Martin Lapointe hit the right post on a breakaway shortly after serving a tripping penalty at 18:43 of the first period. Lapointe then scored his first goal of the game with a shot between goalie Ron Hextall's legs, giving the Wings a 3-1 lead at 19:00 of the first period.

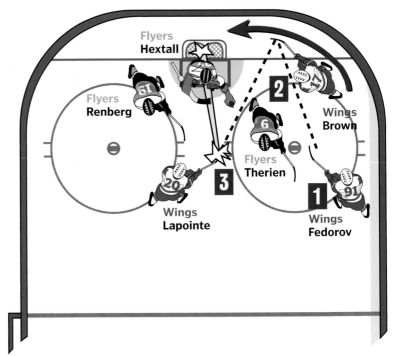

1 After Lapointe (20) hit the post, the Wings kept the puck in the Flyers' zone. Sergei Fedorov (91) got the puck near the right circle and pushed a pass ahead to Doug Brown (17).

2 Heading behind the net, Brown passed out front to Lapointe.

3 Standing in the slot between the Flyers' Mikael Renberg (19) and Chris Therien (6), Lapointe blasted a wrist shot past Hextall (27).

as he exited the penalty box and broke in alone. He fired it off the right post but — ah, persistence — immediately planted himself in front, awaited a beautiful pass from Doug Brown and beat Hextall to make it 3-1.

"We have to find a way to stop the bleeding, this is an embarrassment," said distraught Coach Terry Murray, who must know now that the Flyers are horribly flawed, and the Wings sense the kill. We have seen it so many times, with 13 victories in their

last 15 games. They're all about business, never let up, keep shooting until you see the dead in their eyes.

Shine the Cup and clear the mantle. After 42 years for the franchise, 14 years for the captain, the wait is down to three periods. We expect the Flyers to show up Saturday night, although we're not sure why.

They're merely the wait staff at the biggest party, four decades in the planning and the dreaming, three periods from popping the corks and the ghosts.

Martin Lapointe introduces the Flyers' Janne Niinimaa to the boards at Joe Louis Arena.

WINGS CAN TASTE CUP

By Cynthia Lambert

The Detroit News

When Wings players went to sleep Thursday night, visions of hoisting the Stanley Cup likely were dancing in their heads.

On Saturday night at Joe Louis Arena, they can turn those dreams into reality, thanks to a 6-1 victory over the Philadelphia Flyers in Game 3 of the Stanley Cup Finals. The Wings lead the best-of-seven series three games to none.

"How can you not dream about it?" Darren McCarty said, his smile never fading. "You do that when you're a kid and you're going to do it now. We've put ourselves in a position to fulfill a lot of our dreams. But we also realize that's going to take a lot of hard work."

In the third period, Darren McCarty upends Janne Niinimaa. McCarty drew two interference penalties in Game 3.

Possibly just one more night of work if the Wings can complete a sweep of the Flyers on Saturday. Only once in the Finals has a team lost a series after taking a three-games-to-none lead. In 1942, the Wings took a 3-0 lead before Toronto rallied to win the series.

"We can't think we have four chances to win one game," forward Tomas Sandstrom said. "No team in the league is going to lay down and say, 'Go ahead. Take it.'"

In playoff hockey, the fourth victory is the toughest. Part of the reason is no team — even one as outplayed as the Flyers were Thursday night — will go through the motions. Also, visions of victory can sometimes hamper a team instead of inspire it.

"We've addressed it already, right after the game," assistant coach Mike Krushelnyski said. "Scotty (Bowman) said it and Stevie (Yzerman) said it. It's always toughest to get the final win. As a player, you have to block it out of your mind."

Yzerman said nervous feelings are hard to contain, but the team is focused on preventing them from taking over.

"I think our team has done a good job at getting prepared to play and remaining focused on playing and keeping our minds on hockey," Yzerman said. "We're enjoying ourselves, but again, it's a nerve-racking time."

Said Brendan Shanahan: "We're a team that's on a mission and it's not complete. You've got to battle (the thoughts) out of your mind."

Fighting that will be tougher than the front the Flyers put up Thursday night. Except for a power-play goal by John LeClair at 7:03 of the first period, the Flyers couldn't convert on their chances. The Wings gave them three

Wings defenseman Vladimir Konstantinov takes Flyers forward Trent Klatt into the glass.

more power plays in the first, and the Flyers had a two-man advantage for 1:20 after the Wings got goals from Steve Yzerman (power play) and Sergei Fedorov.

"In the first period, it seemed like a lot of bad things happened to us," Bowman said. "But we got some big goals."

Martin Lapointe scored his first of the game with a minute left in the first to give the Wings a 3-1 lead. As they had done earlier in the series, the Wings got an early goal in the second to squelch the Flyers' hopes of a comeback.

Fedorov got a power-play goal at 3:12 of the second, and Shanahan scored from one of his favorites spots — behind the net — at 19:12, banking the puck off Ron Hextall's knee to make it 5-1.

In the third, the Wings scored quickly — Lapointe again — to end the Flyers' night.

"We've got to find a way to stop the bleeding," Flyers Coach Terry Murray said. "The game was an embarrassment. We've got to give a better effort. The number of odd-man rushes against us was probably in double digits again. That's really unacceptable. We need to get our heads square and start thinking better. Right now, we all need some confidence. We really need to stick together as a team. We've been through hard times before, but you hate to see it in the Stanley Cup Finals."

Whether the Flyers, who look uninspired and defeated, can make a last stand remains to be seen. Whether the Wings can close the series at home Saturday night also is unknown.

But the Wings have been good at clinching in the playoffs this year. They ended series against St. Louis and Anaheim on their first try, and against Colorado on their second.

On the few occasions the Flyers could mount a threat on the Detroit goal, such as this rush by Dainius Zubrus, Mike Vernon and his defensive mates were there to smother the puck.

A Red Wings fan, who has dubbed himself Joe Spirit, pumps up the Joe Louis crowd while parading a homemade Stanley Cup through the stands.

FINALLY!

Wings sweep away Flyers — and demons — to become champions

BY BOB WOJNOWSKI

The Detroit News

AT THE END OF THE LONGEST WAIT, AFTER THE MAGICAL GOAL BY Darren McCarty and the splendid goaltending by Mike Vernon and the nightlong release of emotions raw and real, there was only one more thing to do, and only one person to do it.

GAME 4

Red Wings

2

Flyers

1

at Detroit
June 7, 1997

After the longest wait, the longest skate. Captain Steve Yzerman finally hoisted the Stanley Cup on Saturday night, and as he skated, starting at center ice, slowly toward one goal, then to the other, he shook the silver trophy again and again, perhaps to make sure it was real. Around the rink he went, raising the Cup to every section, every fan, shaking loose theyears of disappointment, and the noise will ring forever.

Darren McCarty scored the winning goal at 13:02 of the second period.

Game Four: Where the Wings shot from

● Goal   ● Shot

The Red Wings outscored the Flyers by one in Game 4 and also outshot them by one, 28-27. Here is a breakdown of the Wings' shots.

No.	Player	Shots
2	Slava Fetisov	2
5	Nicklas Lidstrom	5
14	Brendan Shanahan	3
18	Kirk Maltby	1
19	Steve Yzerman	2
20	Martin Lapointe	1
25	Darren McCarty	2
26	Joe Kocur	2
28	Tomas Sandstrom	1
33	Kris Draper	1
55	Larry Murphy	2
91	Sergei Fedorov	6

Period 1

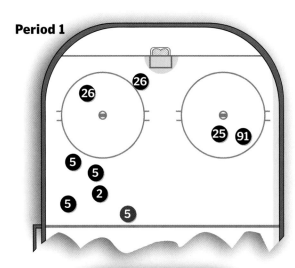

Period 2

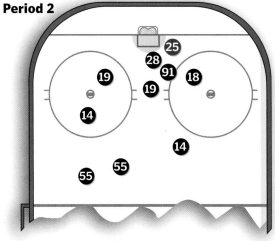

Period 3

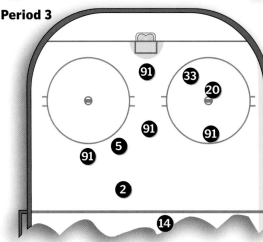

This was a 41-year drought that had become the singular obsession of a city, a team and a man. The wait is over, the weight is lifted, the nightmares end.

"Sometimes you hold your dreams way out there and you wonder if it can ever be as good as you dream," Yzerman said. "It was almost like I wanted to sit back and watch it all and not miss a minute of it."

And those repeated shakes of the Cup?

Yzerman smiled.

"The thing was getting heavy. My arms were giving out."

They were the only parts that ever gave out, as Yzerman's passion sparked a franchise and took it where it hadn't been since 1955. The captain had a cause, and this morning, the Red Wings have the Cup, and sometime around mid-July, the Philadelphia Flyers might recognize what hit them. Spurred by emotion and talent and the relentless red tide of history, the Wings skated through all barriers and took the trophy they had to have.

They won it the only way they could, with contributions from every man on the roster, with Vernon stopping every Philadelphia foray, with all four lines and every defensemen making plays when they had to be made. There was Nicklas Lidstrom, the quiet blue-liner, breaking the tension and the scoreless tie late in the first period with a vicious slap shot. There was McCarty, perhaps the team's most underrated player, grabbing the puck and faking defenseman Janne Niinimaa and then faking goalie Ron Hextall and then sprawling to the ice as he scored.

That was the prettiest snapshot from the Wings' 2-1 victory that offi-

cially broomed the Flyers, and it was framed by players so determined and dominant, it was scary. Vernon, the playoff MVP, was the man who made the important plays on this night, stopping 26 shots and capping a phenomenal playoff run. Scotty Bowman was the general behind the bench, making history by winning his seventh Cup with his third franchise, something no one has ever done.

When it was over, the 63-year-old legend donned skates and took a spin with the Cup himself, something else he had never done.

"I always wanted to be an NHL player and skate with the Cup, and you never know how many chances you'll get," he said. "So I figured I'd go for it. It was pretty heavy, but light, too."

If Bowman was the man with the whip, the captain was the guy who kept it all together, who stood up and spoke when necessary, who was always there, through the lean years and mean years, when he was the only commodity this franchise had.

Now, Yzerman is surrounded by the finest collection of hockey players in the world, and although his scoring role has diminished, his impact never did. It's funny, when he finally gets to smile the broadest, he's missing a tooth, the second dislodging of his career. He gave sweat and blood and teeth and this is why he stayed all these years, 14 in all, through disappointment after disappointment, injury after injury, trade rumor after trade rumor, to take that skate.

He needed a prodding from Brendan Shanahan to begin the longest skate, and when he was done, he handed the Cup to Slava Fetisov and Igor Larionov, the two Russian legends.

Let the celebration begin: Brendan Shanahan was up in arms after the Wings ended their Stanley Cup drought.

"I kind of wanted to do it as a team," Yzerman said, "but it was kind of neat to do it alone."

These Wings did nothing alone, but the "Ste-vie! Ste-vie!" chants will ring the longest, and finally, the cheering wasn't a sentimental gesture for hard work in troubled times, but appreciation for taking a championship team the final step.

Yzerman is the symbol, the lasting image, but he's not a singular star, and that's what makes these Wings unique. They have so many viable components, from the power-skating Sergei Fedorov, to the playmaking Larionov, to the powerful Shanahan, to big-bodied bangers such as McCarty, Martin Lapointe, Kirk Maltby and Joey Kocur. They have punch along the blue line with Nicklas Lidstrom and Vladimir Konstantinov and savvy veterans in Larry Murphy and Fetisov.

This is a team with so many factions on the ice, few off it. And make no mistake. It was bonded by that March 26 game against Colorado, when McCarty did what he had to do, pounding the life out of Claude Lemieux, pounding it into the Wings.

The Wings had a cause, just like the captain. They erased the stink of their playoff humblings and convinced themselves something special was possible. Now, no more questions, no more sad explanations. No more reminiscing about the good ol' days when the Wings won all those championships back in the '50s. The good ol' days are now, resurrected by a team that could not, would not be denied.

Grab a broom and sweep out the old nightmares. Stanley finally came home, delivered by a captain with a cause, and a team that finally found its way.

Hot goaltending has crowd chanting 'Vernie'

Stanley Cup MVPs

Year	Name	Team
1965	Jean Beliveau	Montreal
1966	*Roger Crozier	Red Wings
1967	Dave Keon	Toronto
1968	*Glenn Hall	St. Louis
1969	Serge Savard	Montreal
1970	Bobby Orr	Boston
1971	Ken Dryden	Montreal
1972	Bobby Orr	Boston
1973	Yvan Cournoyer	Montreal
1974	Bernie Parent	Philadelphia
1975	Bernie Parent	Philadelphia
1976	*Reggie Leach	Philadelphia
1977	Guy Lafleur	Montreal
1978	Larry Robinson	Montreal
1979	Bob Gainey	Montreal
1980	Bryan Trottier	New York
1981	Butch Goring	New York
1982	Mike Bossy	New York
1983	Bill Smith	New York
1984	Mark Messier	Edmonton
1985	Wayne Gretzky	Edmonton
1986	Patrick Roy	Montreal
1987	*Ron Hextall	Philadelphia
1988	Wayne Gretzky	Edmonton
1989	Al MacInnis	Calgary
1990	Bill Ranford	Edmonton
1991	Mario Lemieux	Pittsburgh
1992	Mario Lemieux	Pittsburgh
1993	Patrick Roy	Montreal
1994	Brian Leetch	NY Rangers
1995	Claude Lemieux	New Jersey
1996	Joe Sakic	Colorado
1997	**Mike Vernon**	Red Wings

* Played on losing team in the finals.

BY JERRY GREEN

The Detroit News

As Mike Vernon flipped and stopped another puck with his body on the ice, a guy in the lower bowl at Joe Louis Arena waved the sign of the season:

"VERNON I APOLOGIZE."

Of course, the sign had another message written on the opposite side — sort of a two-faced sign.

The same hockey connoisseurs who have been chanting "Vernie, Vernie, Vernie" these past few weeks in the Red Wings' stampede to the Stanley Cup are the same who condemned Vernon two years ago.

Vernon was brilliant again as the Red Wings clinched the Cup for the first time in 42 years with Saturday night's 2-1 victory in a sweep of the Flyers.

"I saw the sign, and I kind of chuckled," Vernon said after he received the Conn Smythe Trophy as the most valuable player in the playoffs. "It was in the back of the minds of all of us, two years ago and how devastating it was to lose to Jersey.

"I don't know who the guy was, but I accept the apology."

Early on, he kept the Red Wings in the game, foiling shot after shot as Philadelphia had a 6-1 advantage in shots. It was the

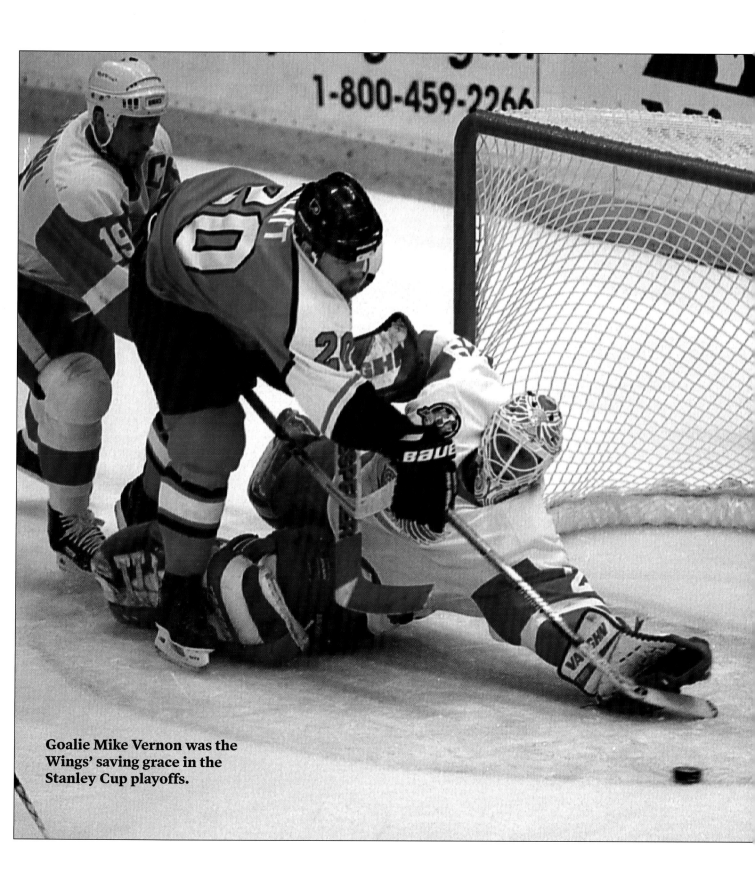

1-800-459-2266

Goalie Mike Vernon was the Wings' saving grace in the Stanley Cup playoffs.

Flyers' heaviest pressure of the series. In one sequence the Flyers surrounded him. The puck went high and Vernon outreached the brawnier Flyers to grab the puck.

And then he thwarted clear shots by Mikael Renberg, Janne Niinimaa and Colin Forbes as the Flyers sought to overhaul the Wings and salvage the game. The Flyers couldn't score until the last 14.8 seconds of the game, with electricity crackling in the building, when Eric Lindros finally got his only goal of the series.

Vernon boosted his playoff record to 16-4, three victories more than he had in the regular season.

Some difference from two years ago in the Finals, the devastation Vernon couldn't forget.

Back then the complaint was a porous 5-hole. The critics recognized that the sweeping Devils blasted too many radar-controlled pucks between Vernon's pads.

Then again, they are the same faithful who welcomed him when he joined the Red Wings via trade from the Calgary Flames in 1994. That was shortly after they chased Tim Chevaldae out of town with their constant jeers.

The key to winning in the playoffs, to winning the Cup itself, is hot goaltending. Hockey ancients swear that is true, citing hot goaltenders of yesteryear such as Terry Sawchuk, Jacques Plante, Gump Worsley, Ken Dryden and, yes, Patrick Roy.

Vernon got hot at the right time.

"Yeah, it is a big challenge for Mike," Red Wings' Coach Scotty Bowman had said to the media.

"... he had a big challenge when he came into Detroit and our goaltending at the time was maligned quite a bit. Some justified and some unjustified ... He bounces back pretty well."

Bounces back indeed.

After all, Bowman, with his habit of tinkering with his goalies, snubbed Vernon through most of the regular season. But Bowman has a sense of hockey history with its hot-goalie theory. In February, Bowman started priming the Red Wings for the playoffs. He started playing Vernon in preference over Chris Osgood. How many nights had the fans chanted: "Ozzie, Ozzie, Ozzie," as Vernon sat dressed in his hockey armor, ignored on the bench?

Vernon was on the brink of becoming the 13th goaltender in NHL history to win 300 games. It was an elusive milestone. In March, he hyperextended a knee in a loss to Anaheim. He missed four games. When he returned in Chicago on March 23, the Blackhawks fired four shots at him. Three went in. Bowman yanked him 7:19 into the first period.

Then came the bloody night of March 26 against Colorado. When the brawling started, Vernon sped out and nailed Roy. He gave away 27 pounds and three inches to Roy. When the fight ended, it was Roy who bled.

It was a simple matter of guts.

And when the game ended in overtime, Vernon had his 300th victory at last. In tribute, Roy, his rival for nearly a dozen years, dispatched the winning puck down ice to Vernon, a souvenir.

McCARTY'S GOAL IS GAME 4 HIGHLIGHT

Darren McCarty put some moves on goalie Ron Hextall, and deftly flicked the puck into the net.

BY DAVE DYE

The Detroit News

When Darren McCarty scores a goal like he did Saturday night, you know it's time to start engraving the names on the Stanley Cup.

McCarty's third goal in 20 playoff games gave the Red Wings a two-goal lead on the way to a Cup-clinching 2-1 victory over the Philadelphia Flyers.

This was not the typical goal that McCarty scores, at least not since he was a peewee. It was the kind that Steve Yzerman or Sergei Fedorov scores. Or Wayne Gretzky or Mario Lemieux.

Who knew Darren McCarty had moves like that?

Certainly not Flyers defenseman Janne Niinimaa, who was so embarrassed and frustrated that he whacked his stick on the crossbar.

McCarty skated up on a rush, used a deke move and went to his left to get around Niinimaa, who fell to the ice. Then he carried the puck back to his right side and around goalie Ron Hextall.

"Every blind squirrel finds a nut," McCarty said while spraying champagne during the dressing-room celebration.

"It's happy, happy job," he said as he hugged teammate Joe Kocur. "Indescribable. Show me the money. Show me the Cup.

"No more '55. Now it's '97. This is what it's all about. We've worked hard all year. It's a great bunch of guys.

"This isn't just for us. It's for the city of Detroit, all our fans who stuck behind us."

The Wings scored many soft goals against the Flyers in the Finals. But McCarty's belongs on the highlight reel for the ages.

"I think he had to dream that one up," Kocur said.

Said Kirk Maltby: "That goal was definitely the turning point for this game."

McCarty, the Wings' second pick (46th overall) in the 1992 draft, first came up to the NHL because of his ability to be an enforcer-type player and fight. But he's shown he can be productive in other ways, too, which is why he took on a larger role this season after the Wings traded other forwards such as Dino Ciccarelli.

McCarty, 25, had a career-best 49 points in the regular season. He had six points in the playoffs this year, and has 21 in his career (11 goals). He scored the winning goal in a pivotal 5-2 victory in Game 5 of the first round against St. Louis.

McCarty also scored the biggest goal of the regular season, when he beat Patrick Roy in overtime for a 6-5 victory in the memorable March 26 game against Colorado.

In that game, he also beat up Claude Lemieux as payback for his hit on Draper in last season's playoff. That night is considered a turning point for the Wings' season.

"Max has been doing this for us all year long," Draper said. "He scored huge goals for us in the playoffs and now, obviously, tonight is icing on the cake.

"It is good to see a guy like that get a big goal in a big game. Everyone loves him in the dressing room. You can tell by the reaction when he scored."

McCarty could barely wait for Saturday night to get there. After Thursday's Game 3 victory, he said it would be a dream come true.

"I'd like to play right now," McCarty said as he was bouncing up and down.

Saturday morning, about nine hours before game time, McCarty said, "If you can't get up for this game, you might as well be six feet under."

"This has been great for the whole community," McCarty said of the interest in the Wings. "It's a great thing. It's bringing a lot of people together. Instead of giving people the finger when they cut you off on the highway, people are now saying, 'OK, you go ahead.' It's a great thing to see."

When the clock struck zero Saturday night on the Joe Louis Arena scoreboard, about 10:50 p.m, McCarty threw off his gloves. He grabbed his helmet and flipped it in the air. Then he raced for the wild celebration at the Wings' net.

It was no longer a dream. It was a Stanley Cup championship for Darren McCarty, the man with more moves than anyone had ever seen before.

McCarty seals it

With smooth moves, Darren McCarty gave the Wings a 2-0 lead in their Stanley Cup-clinching win. Here's how he did it:

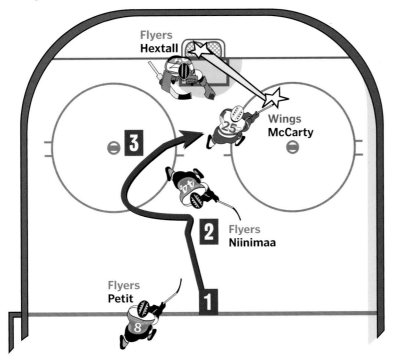

1 Before taking a big hit from the Flyers' Eric Lindros (88), Tomas Sandstrom (28) found Darren McCarty (25) open in the neutral zone. His pass hit McCarty just before McCarty hit center ice.

2 As he gained the Flyers' zone, McCarty was met by Flyers defenseman Janne Niinimaa (44), with defenseman Michel Petit (8) trailing on the play.

3 McCarty faked out Niinimaa by going to his left, then back to his right. Flyers goalie Ron Hextall (27) tried to halt McCarty by moving to his right, but McCarty pulled the puck back and went to Hextall's left and scored with a wrist shot at 13:02 of the second period.

WINGS TAKE FLIGHT IN CUP FINALE

Wings captain Steve Yzerman hoists the Stanley Cup toward team owners Mike and Marian Ilitch.

BY CYNTHIA LAMBERT

The Detroit News

The Red Wings will no longer use memories of failing in the playoffs as their motivation.

Now they have the real thing — success and the Stanley Cup.

In convincing fashion, the Wings claimed their first Stanley Cup since 1955 with a 2-1 victory over the Philadelphia Flyers on Saturday night at Joe Louis Arena, sweeping them out of town in four games.

The prestigious trophy was presented by NHL Commissioner Gary Bettman to captain Steve Yzerman, who hoisted it over his head for everyone to see. After spending 14 years as the leader and inspiration of this team, Yzerman finally could discard all the failures and hold high hockey's most prized possession.

"I don't know how to describe how I feel," Yzerman said. "I'm glad the game is over, but I wish it never ended."

Yzerman shared the trophy and the accomplishment with his teammates, particularly goaltender Mike Vernon, who appeared in every playoff game this year, going 16-4.

Vernon also was rewarded with the Conn Smythe Trophy, presented to the playoff MVP. He had a 1.79 goals-against average in the playoffs and a .944 save percentage in the Finals.

Throughout this postseason, the Wings had talked of how losing to New Jersey in the 1995 Finals, when they were swept, and the Western Conference finals to Colorado last season was their motivation. And as each opponent — St. Louis, Anaheim and then Colorado — was dispatched in this postseason, the Wings gained momentum. By the time they faced the Flyers, their game was honed.

"The experience of the last two years was huge," Wings Coach Scotty Bowman said. "The team was more prepared."

Bowman, who won his seventh Cup with an NHL-record third team, said he has not decided whether he will return next season as head coach. He said he would like to leave the game the way his idol, Toe Blake, did. Blake, who won eight Cups with Montreal, retired after leading the Canadiens to the 1968 title.

As they did in each of the previous three games of the series, the Wings scored on a long shot. On Saturday night, Nicklas Lidstrom beat Ron Hextall with a shot from the blue line at 19:27 of the first period. Darren McCarty made it 2-0 at 13:02 of the second period on a fabulous rush. He made enough moves to leave the Flyers' defense helpless and Hextall far out of the net.

With 14.8 seconds left, Eric Lindros scored for the Flyers, who had pulled Hextall with 1:48 left for an extra attacker.

The Wings led 1-0 after the first period on Lidstrom's goal. They started strongly in the second, initiating the play instead of reacting. But the score remained tight.

That is, until The Rush.

With the puck at the boards in the Wings' zone, Tomas Sandstrom withstood a hit to make a perfect pass to McCarty beyond the blue line. McCarty sped through the neutral zone and into the Flyers' end. Defenseman Janne Niinimaa stood between McCarty and Hextall, but McCarty took care of that with a quick move to the left that sent Niinimaa spinning to the ice.

McCarty drew Hextall out to the left, pulled the puck to his forehand and cut right. McCarty's move was so quick that Hextall was still out of the crease when the shot went into an open net at 13:02.

What was McCarty thinking about during his rush?

"I don't know," he said. "I think I moved to the right and lost the puck, so then I headed left. Before I knew it, I was right on Hextall.

"Don't expect that all the time."

Sergei Fedorov, right, led the Wings with six points in the Finals.

FEDOROV'S TOUGH SEASON ENDS WITH A FLOURISH

BY JOHN NIYO

The Detroit News

He already had the fancy skates. He already had the fancy commercials. He already had the fancy car.

Soon now, Sergei Fedorov will have the fancy ring, too. Diamonds are forever, eh, Sergei?

His smile Saturday night said it all, embellishing his statistics — three goals and three assists in the Finals, eight goals and 12 assists overall.

Not a bad way to finish what has been, in Fedorov's words, his "most difficult season."

Fedorov, 27, is in the final year of his contract. And, fresh off last year's playoff disappointment, he and his agent, Mike Barnett, spent the better part of the early months this season haggling over Fedorov's worth with the Red Wings organization.

There were brief glimpses of this former Hart Trophy winner — most notably that five-goal performance

Dec. 26 against Washington, when he scored all the Wings' goals in a 5-4 overtime victory.

But more often, Fedorov was a portrait of unhappiness, struggling to find his scoring touch, banished to Scotty Bowman's checking line and quietly fuming at the insult.

At one point, he remarked that the third-line status was "an honor," although everyone within earshot could detect the sarcasm.

Then came Bowman's experiment late in the season, when he switched Fedorov to defense, even starting the playoffs with this Nike poster boy on the blue line.

Again, Fedorov kept quiet, or at least relatively so. He said he was happy getting more minutes — as many as 30 a game — and shrugged off questions about his winter of discontent.

"I mean, he's a different person," said teammate Darren McCarty, whose locker is next to Fedorov's in the dressing room. "That's what some people don't understand. He's not like everybody else.

"Compared to me, I'm more out-going, more emotional, a scream-and-yell guy. Sergei is more to himself. People can't read him."

Fedorov scored the two most important goals in Game 3 of the Finals — unassisted on the winner in the first period, and with a nifty move for the Wings' fourth goal to seal it.

"You got to give the guy a break," McCarty said Saturday morning. "He can be the best player in the league when he wants to. He seizes his opportunities. Last game (Game 3 against Philadelphia), he proved it. It was the biggest game of our career, and he rose to the occasion."

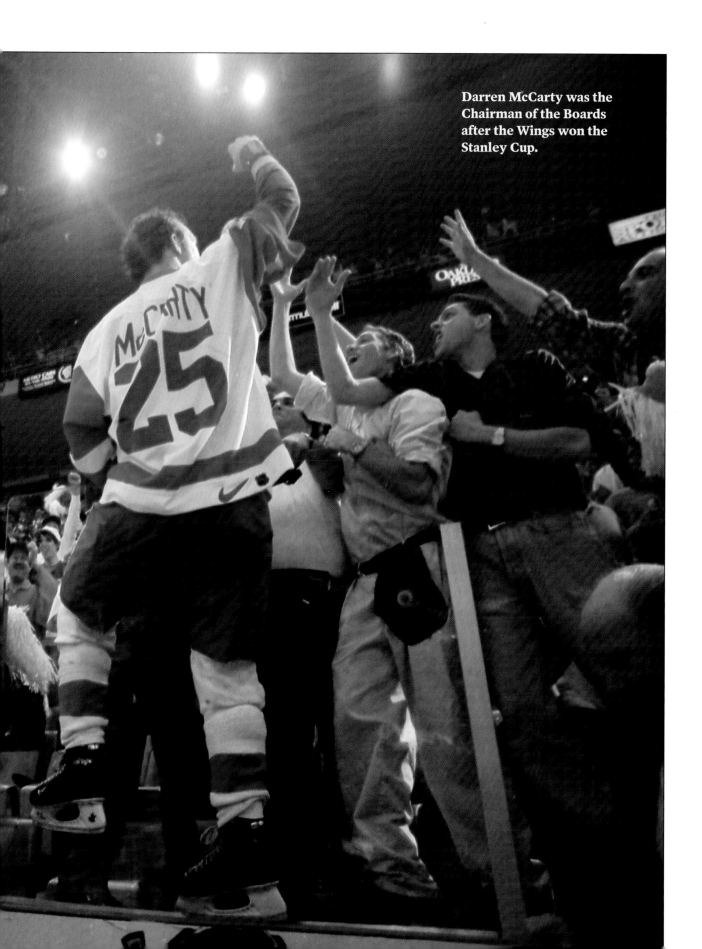

Darren McCarty was the Chairman of the Boards after the Wings won the Stanley Cup.

Stevie Y.

Quiet captain speaks volumes in leading the Wings to the Cup

BY JERRY GREEN

The Detroit News

A nd then it happened. The guardians, wearing white gloves, opened the strong box that protected the 104-year-old Stanley Cup. The trophy was set, gleaming in the bright lights, onto the table at center ice. And Steve Yzerman, the Captain, skated over to receive it.

At last, long last.

The confetti floated from the rafters. The Red Wings were Stanley Cup champions, for the first time since 1955, 10 years before Yzerman was born. They had swept the Philadelphia Flyers in four games, with sheer ice control, poise, discipline.

Yzerman hesitated with the Cup, uncertain. And then he raised it toward his teammates and the cheering multitudes. He caressed it and put it above his head again, pumped it upward in triumph. And then he skated around the ice at Joe Louis Arena in the captain's championship lap.

It was a ritual he knew well. He had watched, in envy, for years as Wayne Gretzky and Mario Lemieux and Mark Messier and Joe Sakic, captains of other conquering teams, had taken the Cup on its annual tour around the rink.

"As long as I could remember, since I was 5 years old, I watched the Stanley Cup, I've stayed up, made a point of watching it presented, watched the celebration in the locker room, and always dreamed that maybe I'd get there," Yzerman said.

"But ... and sometimes you wonder if you'll ever get there. So I guess, as the game was going on, and when we

finally won, it's almost like I wanted to sit back and watch the whole thing and not miss a minute of it, and not forget any of it. I don't know if it can ever be as good as the dream, but I'd rather sit back and just watch everybody. I don't want to miss any of it."

Steve Yzerman is a quiet captain. He keeps his emotions harnessed. He seldom shows jubilation, except when he lifts his hockey stick and smiles after scoring a goal. He joined the Red Wings when he was 18. At 21, he was captain of the team. He has suffered the indignity of trade rumors, injury, defeat.

And now, at the end of his 14th sea-

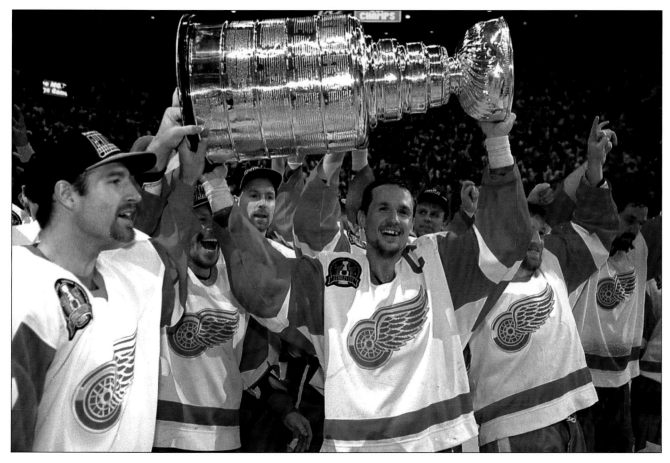

Steve Yzerman finally gets to experience the Stanley Cup presentation he had always watched on television.

son, he had his grip on the Stanley Cup. At last. He began his solo skate, slowly, searching into the grandstands, into the multitudes.

"I was looking for my parents," he said. "And then I was looking for my wife in the corner."

He toured to the far side of the rink, to the roar of the crowd, as his team waited for him to return.

"The thing was getting heavy," Yzerman said. "My arms were giving out."

He skated around and handed the Cup to Slava Fetisov, one of the Red Wings' celebrated and sometimes maligned, Russian Five. Fetisov is

pushing 40, a defenseman whose craggy face displayed a series of stick scars from more than 20 years of high-level hockey wars. He had won Olympic and world championships for the Soviet Union. He played for the renowned Red Army team, or CSKA, in Moscow. Then with bitterness, he broke with the Red Army team and led the stream of Russian hockey defectors to North America — just as communism collapsed and the Soviet Union fragmented.

It was to Fetisov that Captain Yzerman handed the trophy to begin the tradition in which every player has his turn to hoist, kiss and cherish

the Cup. Fetisov placed one side of the Cup into the hands of Igor Larionov, his 36-year-old teammate with the Red Army and the Red Wings. They skated in tandem with the Cup.

Through the years of the Red Wings' failures to win, critics had faulted the Russians for not comprehending the spirit of the Stanley Cup.

"As far as giving it to Slava," said Yzerman, "the last couple of days — you try not to think about anything but the game, you've got a million things running through your mind, and I got caught up with who should I hand the Cup off to?"

Always a potent shot, Yzerman had to change his game under Coach Scotty Bowman. Without complaint and despite the critics, he traded points for victories.

"I thought of a few different players. Slava jumped to my mind because of what he's done. He and Igor, what kind of guys they are. I really respect them, what they've done and how they've handled themselves, and they set an example in their work ethic and their attitude for the young Russian players. And they've been real leaders on our team.

"I don't know if Slava's coming back next year or not. But after the great career he's had I wanted him to get the trophy. He's done everything in the world of hockey, and this is the most important thing, so I wanted to give it to him."

The symbolism was captured. Steve Yzerman, through the years, had been a captain criticized often for not being loud or sufficiently vocal in his leadership. He explained so often that he stresses leadership by example.

Part of his quiet front is shyness. Part of it is modesty. He was born in British Columbia, grew up in Nepean, Ontario, in suburban Ottawa. He was raised well in citizenship. He was raised well in hockey.

Seldom has he rebuked his teammates. But he did in the first round of the 1997 playoffs, when they were deadlocked after a 4-0 loss to St. Louis. He stood up and challenged his team, urging them to start producing. He included himself in the criticism.

Seldom has he jabbed at a player. But in the 1997 series with Colorado, Sergei Fedorov rode into the boards, damaging his ribs. Fedorov could barely breath. He was assisted to the dressing room. He was considered done for the game. Yzerman approached him after the first period: "Sergei, we need you." Fedorov soon returned. He was brilliant when he got back. He scored the winning goal

Yzerman challenged and prodded his teammates during the playoffs. His speech after a loss to St. Louis in the opening series sparked the Wings.

that eliminated the Avalanche.

Seldom has he engaged in hockey's rough stuff, the fighting. But one night, years ago when a brawl broke out, Yzerman was seen punching the Canadiens' Bobby Smith in a corner of the Forum.

It is leadership.

And as Yzerman led, each of the Red Wings did his bit with the Stanley Cup. Even Scotty Bowman, with his seventh Stanley Cup championship as a coach, put on his skates to ride with the trophy. Then the Cup was taken from the ice. It was transported into the Red Wings dressing room, into the back, where on the stationary bikes Yzerman had pedaled for hours, days, restrengthening muscle from his various injuries.

The bandwagon rolled into the champions' dressing room soon after the Cup. Folks who had recently discovered that water freezes at 32

degrees Fahrenheit to form ice poured into the room. It was jammed, sweltering from the TV lights, champagne spraying around the room, drenching the red shirts and dresses of the interlopers.

Yzerman stood out front among the crowd. His face was soaked with sweat. He had the very beginnings of another playoff goatee on his chin and cheeks. He had stripped off his No. 19 jersey with the captain's C on the left front shoulder. He wore a cap that read: "Stanley Cup CHAMPS." And he patiently endeavored to deliver the feelings of his past frustrations to the media marvels who were about to reach him. Mostly, he expressed relief — that it was his turn and he was relishing it.

"I love this team," he said.

"I was going to feel all this different stuff. It happened too quick. When I started playing as a kid, I dreamed of

Yzerman, 32, has been in the spotlight with the Red Wings for 14 seasons. He was named captain of the team at the age of 21.

the NHL and the Stanley Cup. But it was filled with a lot of disappointments ... a lot of tough losses. I think I'm a better player for it.

"The hardest part is sitting around waiting. I can usually sleep the afternoon before a game. I couldn't today. I just wanted to be left alone. Let's get on the ice and play.

"We've had some disappointments and we've broken people's hearts. People would always say, as good as you are, you didn't win the Cup.

"Now people can't say that."

Yzerman spoke as the bedlam went on around him. It was after midnight, early Sunday morning. Brendan Shanahan came up and spoke words into Yzerman's ear. Shanahan was still dressed in full game regalia, his No. 14 jersey, his ice skates.

A half dozen mini tape recorders nearly brushed Yzerman's whiskers. Some reporters stood in the second circle around him, scratching his words into their notebooks. Fans pushed in.

They, the hockey fans, are passionate people. In Detroit, they are vigorously devoted to their team. They are fickle, of course. In the few years past they had rabidly cheered the Red Wings when they had hugely successful regular seasons, then were defeated in the playoffs. They felt disgraced when the Red Wings went out in the first round to the ancient-rival Maple Leafs one year, then the upstart San Jose Sharks the next. They bled and cursed when the Red Wings reached the Stanley Cup

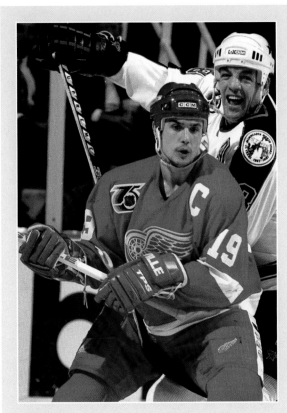

Yzerman's career numbers

Year	Team	Regular Season					Playoffs				
		GP	G	A	P	PM	GP	G	A	P	PM
1983-84	Detroit	80	39	48	87	33	4	3	3	6	0
1984-85	Detroit	80	30	59	89	58	3	2	1	3	2
1985-86	Detroit	51	14	28	42	16	-	-	-	-	-
1986-87	Detroit	80	31	59	90	43	16	5	13	18	8
1987-88	Detroit	64	50	52	102	44	3	1	3	4	6
1988-89	Detroit	80	65	90	155	61	6	5	5	10	2
1989-90	Detroit	79	62	65	127	79	-	-	-	-	-
1990-91	Detroit	80	51	57	108	34	7	3	3	6	4
1991-92	Detroit	79	45	58	103	64	11	3	5	8	12
1992-93	Detroit	84	58	79	137	44	7	4	3	7	4
1993-94	Detroit	58	24	58	82	36	3	1	3	4	0
1994-95	Detroit	47	12	26	38	40	15	4	8	12	0
1995-96	Detroit	80	36	59	95	64	18	8	12	20	4
1996-97	Detroit	81	22	63	85	78	20	7	6	13	4
TOTAL		**1,023**	**539**	**801**	**1,340**	**694**	**113**	**46**	**65**	**111**	**46**

Finals for the first time in 29 years in 1995, then were swept in four games by the New Jersey Devils. And they vilified their team when the Red Wings were defeated in 1996 in the bitter Western Conference final series by the hated Colorado Avalanche.

Yzerman was among those condemned by anonymous fans, callers to sports talk shows: "He never turns up for the playoffs." "He's always hurt."

Uncontrolled rumors abounded that the Red Wings would trade him.

"The last five years, you didn't want to be recognized," Yzerman said to his audience. "I put a hat on, glasses on. You don't want people to recognize you.

"A couple of years ago I went to Las Vegas after the playoffs. I don't remember which year. I was at the craps table. Two old guys from Windsor came by and saw me. They said, 'You don't want to play at this table. There's no luck at this table.' "

About that time, Yzerman sat with a single reporter in a rare interview, speaking his inner feelings.

"Yeah, always," he said about watching the Stanley Cup presentation ceremony on television in his home in suburban Detroit each spring. "You're driving down the road and some song comes on the radio and you're thinking about it. I've always thought about that, every year.

"Every year I've always tried, no matter what I'm doing, no matter what I've seen or missed of the playoffs, I always try to make a point of seeing the final game — or the end of the final game — because I enjoy see-

ing the Stanley Cup presented.

"I enjoy seeing the Super Bowl, or the world championship in baseball or basketball.

"I like seeing the finish part. Yeah, I think everybody, whatever they dream of, always pictures it the same way.

"I've got friends who've won the Cup, and it's interesting to see people when they win and how they react. To see them in the summer and ask what it was like. Just to see what it's like ...

"Very envious ...

"I found that the last couple of years, as the hype and expectation for our team has grown, there are setbacks along the way. And although they seem the end of the world at the time, you survive, improve and improve, and at some point, you get to reach your goal.

"But every year, as we've kind of faded in the playoffs, it grows a little more imperative — I guess in my mind — to accomplish what you want to accomplish."

Now, after 14 years, mature at 32, he had accomplished what he wanted to accomplish. He did it as a player who had been required to adjust his style, make alternate use of his skills.

Through his first 10 seasons in Detroit, Yzerman's primary function was to score goals. He became one of the more prolific scorers in the NHL. He ranked in stature with Gretzky and Lemieux. He became regarded as the second greatest offensive player in the franchise's history, after only Gordie Howe. In 1988-89, Yzerman scored 65 goals. In other seasons, he scored 62, 58, 51 and 50 goals. Howe had 49 in his best goal-scoring season.

The sport, of course, was different when Howe played it. Schedules were shorter. There were six teams, all skilled. Expansion created a 26-team league, diluted in talent.

But Howe had won the Stanley Cup four times.

When Bowman became the Red Wings' coach in 1993, one of his earliest machinations was to try to recreate Yzerman. Bowman wanted a fast, slick defensive forward, one adept at forechecking. Yzerman never complained. But he did not thrill to the change.

He still scored, but never with the production of the earlier years. So the critics harped. The trade rumors proliferated.

There had been reports that he would be traded after the Red Wings lost in the playoffs in 1994 to San Jose. They vanished without merit.

But such rumors were wildly pounced upon after the Jersey sweep for the Cup in 1995. The Ottawa Senators made an overture for Yzerman. He was a hometown player. They had a general manager, Randy Sexton, who was on the cusp, trying to salvage his job. The Senators had a new rink and needed a name player to lure fans inside. Rumors were floated in Ottawa, printed as a done deal. They were refloated in Detroit.

Yzerman fretted. The Senators were an expansion team with a dubious future. They were mismanaged.

The trade rumors proliferated. Out of character, at a practice session before the season opened in 1995, Yzerman lost his temper. He threw his stick. He barked at the media.

As it turned out, he wasn't traded. The rumors had slammed out of control, based on Ottawa's wishful thinking. Two high-echelon sources on the Red Wings confirmed that an Yzerman trade was never seriously close. Jimmy Devellano, a Detroit club vice-president, said the Red Wings had stacked the price so high for Yzerman that the Senators could never afford to make such a deal.

Two things happened in the aftermath.

Yzerman mused about the media, still miffed.

"Don't they have any accountability?" he said one day.

The second thing that happened was that Mike Ilitch, the club owner, signed him to a contract that bound him to the Red Wings for the duration of his career. It would pay $17.5 million over four seasons, and guaranteed a front-office job when Yzerman retired as a player.

That night, Yzerman celebrated. He had a goal and three assists.

Perhaps, of all the goals he has scored — 539 in the regular season and and 46 in the playoffs — his finest, his most sensational was in the 1996 playoffs. A seven-game struggle with the St. Louis Blues went into double overtime. Yzerman ended it with a blazing shot. He spun around behind the net with all his teammates on top of him, thumping his back.

That would be surpassed by the goal he scored against the Avalanche in the second game of the 1997 Western Conference finals. The Red Wings had lost the first game and had trailed, 2-0, in the second. Quickly, they were in position for another disappointment. Detroit tied it. Yzerman set up Fedorov for the tying goal.

With four minutes left, Yzerman got the puck in the Detroit zone, sped through center, around the Colorado defense. From behind the net he shoved the puck at goalie Patrick Roy. It went in off Roy's leg. It would become the most vital goal of Yzerman's 14 seasons in Detroit.

It turned around the series. From then on, the Red Wings were dominant against Colorado — losing only one more game — and over Philadelphia — losing none. Yzerman had another key goal in the first game of the Finals, the long-distance shot that doomed the Flyers.

Several years ago, the Canadiens signed Patrick Roy to a contract paying $4 million a season. To justify such a sum at that time, Serge Savard, then Canadiens' general manager, explained to Montreal reporters that Roy had won Stanley Cups, "a guy like Yzerman has never won anything."

But now it has happened. The Captain has his Cup.

The Coach

At 63, Bowman changed himself, and changed Wings into winners

BY JERRY GREEN

The Detroit News

I t is a dangerous game. The players carry clubs in their hands. They wear honed steel blades as sharp as knives on their feet. They dash crazily on ice and shoot a galvanized rubber disc wildly at speeds above 100 miles an hour. In an earlier era, they did not wear protective helmets.

It is the game Scotty Bowman aspired to play in the National Hockey League, since he was a wee lad in an English-speaking neighborhood of Montreal. He possessed the talent for the game. It was evident he was NHL material by the time he reached junior hockey in his late teens.

Then — Bowman relishes retelling his life story — the accident that turned him into coaching. He sat one day during hockey season in the back room where the Red Wings coaches view videos and diagram defenses. The room is reporter-proof. A rare

invitation was issued. And he spoke:

"I got my first skates when I was maybe seven. That was pretty young in those days. You didn't get on teams until you were around 12. I got on a team when I was around 10. I played when I was seven, but we didn't have organized teams.

"I got on a group team when I was about 14. We won the whole province of Quebec midget championship."

He advanced to the Montreal Royals, the Canadiens' top junior club. One day, on the ice, there was a collision. Two players carrying those

clubs, riding on those steel knife-sharp blades. Bowman received a severe whack in the head. His skull was shattered. His career ambitions were crushed.

He loved hockey so he steered into coaching, where he would become an immortal. He would coach the great Canadiens to five Stanley Cup champions in his native Montreal. He would coach the Pittsburgh Penguins to another Stanley Cup championship in 1992. And at age 63, after bitter disappointments, he would recreate, mastermind, tinker with the Red

Scotty Bowman embraces Conn Smythe winner Mike Vernon following Game 4.

151

Wings until they were molded into his ideal of a championship team. And they would win the Stanley Cup in 1997 for the first time in 42 years.

Coach of seven Stanley Cup champions, player development director of another, the ironic result of a knock in the head. Only Toe Blake, of the mighty Canadiens in the 1950's and 60's, coached more Stanley Cup champions than Bowman, eight.

"A player was all I wanted to be," he said, continuing his story in the back room in the bowels of Joe Louis Arena. "I went to high school but ... Actually when I got injured, I was still in high school. It was my senior year. I was playing junior hockey. I got injured March 7, 1951. I was 18 ½."

There was a skirmish. Scotty was hit over the head by a stick. He fell to the ice, badly hurt. The player who whacked Bowman over the head with the hockey stick was a young defenseman, Jean-Guy Talbot. Bowman would never forget the name.

Young coaches are required to begin at the bottom, the roots of hockey across Canada. Bowman started with kids' hockey, junior B's, juniors in Ottawa, the Peterborough Petes, the junior Canadiens. In 1967, the NHL expanded, doubled in size from The Original Six. There were six head coaching positions instantly available.

Bowman was hired by Lynn Patrick to coach the new St. Louis Blues.

His players were craggy veterans, their careers prolonged by new job opportunities. Bowman had two brilliant hockey Hall of Famers to play goal, Glenn Hall and Jacques Plante. He had Dickie Moore and Doug Harvey, two aging players from the Canadiens past champions.

But in this first season, Bowman sought another veteran defenseman.

Bowman's NHL record

Year	Team	Regular Season			Playoffs	
		W	L	T	W	L
1967-68	St. Louis	23	21	14	8	10
1968-69	St. Louis	37	25	14	8	4
1969-70	St. Louis	32	7	12	8	8
1970-71	St. Louis	13	10	5	2	4
1971-72	Montreal	46	16	16	2	4
1972-73	Montreal*	52	10	16	12	5
1973-74	Montreal	45	24	9	2	4
1974-75	Montreal	47	14	19	6	5
1975-76	Montreal*	58	11	11	12	1
1976-77	Montreal*	60	8	12	12	2
1977-78	Montreal*	59	10	11	12	3
1978-79	Montreal*	52	17	11	12	4
1979-80	Buffalo	47	17	16	9	5
1981-82	Buffalo	18	10	7	1	3
1982-83	Buffalo	38	28	14	2	3
1983-84	Buffalo	48	25	7	0	3
1984-85	Buffalo	38	28	14	2	3
1985-86	Buffalo	18	18	1	0	0
1986-87	Buffalo	3	7	2	0	0
1991-92	Pittsburgh*	39	32	9	16	5
1992-93	Pittsburgh	56	21	7	7	5
1993-94	Detroit	46	30	8	3	4
1994-95	Detroit	33	11	4	12	6
1995-96	Detroit	62	13	7	10	9
1996-97	Detroit*	36	26	18	16	4
TOTAL		**1.011**	**460**	**263**	**178**	**105**

* Stanley Cup champions

He scanned the NHL's waiver wire. He picked a name.

The player he brought to the blues was an ornery craggy, tough, veteran defenseman. His name was Jean-Guy Talbot.

The irony was rich. They never discussed the incident that had terminated Bowman's career as a player at its beginning 16 years earlier.

He developed the elderly Blues into a team that reached the Stanley Cup Finals the first three years of their existence. The NHL, in its desire

Avalanche Coach Marc Crawford had plenty to say, but Bowman had the last laugh in the Western Conference finals. The Wings beat Colorado in six games to advance to the Stanley Cup Finals.

to market the United States, rigged the playoffs so that an American expansion club would reach the Finals every year. Scotty's Blues never won a game against the established Canadiens or Bruins in three championship series.

But he was established as an NHL coach. His jut-jawed image, head held upward, reaching down for an ice cube to munch, would become a television caricature for more than a quarter century.

Bowman was coveted by Charles O. Finley to coach the California Seals and Jack Kent Cooke to coach the Los Angeles Kings. He rejected both owners. He would ultimately return to Montreal. He had proven, in signing Talbot, that he did not necessarily have to love his players to win. Many of them have proven through the years that they certainly didn't love him.

In Detroit, there was a huge generation gap. Bowman had the credentials, he had the hockey knowledge, but it was uncertain that he had the knack to handle athletes 35 and 40 years younger than he was. He has been successful through the 1960's, an era of young rage, and the 1970's, 80's into the 90's. The character of North American youth changed. Salaries climbed and climbed. Athletes needed pampering. The dressing room often turned into a sandbox.

Plus there was another gap. This gap was transoceanic. The Red Wings were avidly signing

Bowman always wanted to be an NHL star, but after he suffered a head injury during a game, he was forced into switching to another career — coaching.

Europeans. They brought in players from Sweden. When the Soviet Union crumbled in 1989, skillful Russian hockey players suddenly found they were free to become millionaires. The Red Wings quickly signed players from Moscow's famed CSKA champions, the noted Red Army team. They picked off Sergei Fedorov, Vladimir Konstantinov, Vyacheslav Kozlov. All for free. Valerie Gushin, the general manager of the Red Army team in Moscow, cried American piracy. The Red Wings laughed in response.

Bowman handled athletes of mixed personalities, sulkers and carousers, for 25 years in the NHL. But Russians — and the Red Wings would have a Russian Five when they won the Stanley Cup — would be a different sort of challenge.

Sitting in the room, Bowman pointed to one of the five Russians.

"He had a lifestyle orgasm," Bowman said. "He had no idea five years ago he'd have what he has now."

When Bowman arrived in Detroit in 1993, he had just won his sixth Cup as a coach in Pittsburgh. He became the Detroit coach with the simple mandate from franchise owner Mike Ilitch:

"Win the Cup."

It took four seasons of grooming, retooling, cajoling, surviving front office politics — and changing some playing lifestyles. It took four years of carping, and rumors, from much of the media. It took four years of playing goalkeeper tag.

"My idol in hockey was Toe Blake," said Bowman. "But the coach I admired was Don Shula. He lasted a long time. He had to change styles."

But more often, Bowman had been compared to another historic, despotic football coach in moods, temperament, handling of athletes.

"He is the best coach in any sport since Vince Lombardi," a journalist familiar with both eras said during the 1996-97 season.

It was the ultimate compliment.

Bowman's first three seasons with the Red Wings were shocking, disappointing, frustrating, controversial, at times angry.

Ilitch hired Bowman after Jacques Demers and then Bryan Murray were given the ziggy — a Detroit-only word that translates to an unceremonious firing. Demers and Murray had moderate success. Murray spent three years as coach and general manager. After failures in the playoffs, he was replaced by Bowman, but retained the GM's position.

The Red Wings had stars. Bowman inherited Steve Yzerman, the club's captain. At the time, Yzerman was regarded in the same scoring echelon as Mario Lemieux and Wayne Gretzky. Yzerman had seasons in which he had scored 50, 65, 62, 51 and 58 goals.

One of Bowman's first acts was to change Yzerman's style. A swift, elusive skater, Bowman had Yzerman concentrate on defense.

The Red Wings finished first in the Western Conference in Bowman's first season. They were humiliated in the first round of the playoffs by the lightweight San Jose Sharks.

Ilitch impatiently courted Mike Keenan, who had just won the Cup with the Rangers, to switch to Detroit as coach. The Blues outbid the Red Wings for Keenan. Bowman survived.

What the Red Wings had was two coach/GM types, Bowman and Murray. One naturally had to go. Murray was fired. Bowman assumed his basic duties as director of player personnel.

His second season, the Red Wings reached the Cup Finals for the first time in 29 years. Detroit was agog with hockey enthusiasm. The Red Wings were favored to win the Stanley Cup against the New Jersey Devils, once referred to as "a Mickey Mouse team" by Wayne Gretzky. Detroit hadn't won it since 1955. The Devils blew the Red Wings out in a horrendous four-game sweep.

Shawn Burr was made the scapegoat. He was traded to Tampa Bay.

Burr told The St. Petersburg Times what happened once when Bowman called him for an opinion of the coaching.

"Scotty, you're 60 years old," Burr was quoted as saying. "You play with toy trains. You use a duck call to make line changes. People call you a genius. I think there's something wrong with you. I think you're a joke."

In Bowman's third season the Red Wings roared through the schedule. They had a target — the magic sports number of 60. In all of NHL history only one club had won 60 games in a season. It was the 1976-77 Canadiens, coached by Scotty Bowman. It was the second of Bowman's four-season Cup dynasty in Montreal. The Red Wings broke the record with 62 victories.

He can be a secretive man with a deep curiosity.

This time the Red Wings were eliminated in a heated, nasty six-game semifinal, or Western Conference final, series with the Colorado Avalanche. Bowman enraged, engaged in a nasty parking lot shouting match in Denver with the Avalanche's Claude Lemieux.

"Nice sucker punch, Lemieux,"

Don Cherry, left, and Bowman had one thing in common: They each coached a Cup champion.

Bowman was heard to yell from the Red Wings' bus.

For the first time, Marc Crawford, the young Colorado coach, spouted angry remarks at Bowman.

"He's the master of creating a little bit of circus away from the game ..." Crawford told the media.

"He's been doing this thing for years and years and years ...

"He's a great thinker, but he thinks so much that you even get the plate in his head causing interference on our headsets during the game."

It was a cruel remark. One of the myths in the NHL is that Bowman has a plate in his head because of the incident with Talbot.

Some of Bowman's old Montreal players who went on to high posts in hockey spoke with praise. Former All-Star defenseman Larry Robinson is now coach of the Kings.

"Hate is the wrong word, but when he was coaching us, he wasn't a guy you as a player respected," Robinson told the Los Angeles Times. "But you respect him now more that you're through. To you, it's a game. To him, it's much more than that. He's always trying to stay a step ahead. He's constantly thinking of ways to make you a better player. I guess I misunderstood when I was a player. But being in his shoes now, I understand a lot better why he did the things he did."

It was the highest tribute a former player could give to his former coach.

Ken Dryden, Bowman's Montreal goalkeeper, now is boss of the Maple Leafs.

"The only common piece is Scotty Bowman, and that says a lot," Dryden said while the Red Wings were aiming to break the 60-victories record.

Beaten again in the playoffs by Colorado, Bowman again reformed his club for 1996-97. This time the club was created to win the playoffs. The regular season was simply regarded as a testing period. They finished second in the division, third in the conference.

Bowman had a grander scheme. He dealt popular Dino Ciccarelli to Tampa Bay. "He's a jerk," Ciccarelli said publicly. He cashiered Bob Errey.

"A man that doesn't respect people should not be given any respect," Errey told The St.Petersburg Times. "Why would you want time for a man like that."

Bowman shrugged off the criticism.

He dealt Paul Coffey and Keith Primeau to Hartford to obtain a huge property the Red Wings desperately needed — Brendan Shanahan. He brought Joey Kocur back from a suburban Detroit beer league to provide muscle. He played the five Russians as a unit — Fedorov, Kozlov, Igor Larionov, Konstantinov, Slava Fetisov. Then he broke them up. Unlike the year before, when he played guessing games whether Chris Osgood or Mike Vernon would start playoff games, he settled on a single goalkeeper. He relegated the younger Osgood to the bench and went with the experienced Vernon. To shore up the defense, he obtained Larry Murphy from the Maple Leafs.

And when playoffs came, the Red Wings were prepared. They rolled through. They beat St. Louis in six. They swept Anaheim, with three games going into overtime. After a triple overtime victory, Bowman even showed some emotion. He smiled. They evened matters with Colorado, Bowman admonishing Crawford during one evening of belligerence in Joe Louis Arena.

William Scott Bowman, himself, had revered his father. He was the son of a Scottish immigrant in a bilingual city. It is rather difficult to picture Scotty Bowman, as a little boy, playing with the kids down the street, wearing his Boston Bruins' replica jersey, in the 1930's and early 1940's.

Young Scotty Bowman, perverse even as a lad, favored neither the Canadiens nor the Maroons, soon to be disbanded.

"I grew up a Boston Bruin fan," Bowman said in his back room, "the reason being the Boston radio broadcast. You could pick up the signal in Montreal. I think the reason was, I was about seven years old, and they were winning the Cup. The Rangers won it in '40. Boston won it in '41.

"I used to have to go to bed at the end of the first or second period. My father would always write the score before he went to work the next day.

"I think probably the reason that I was a Boston fan, they were a strong team. One Christmas I got ... somehow they found a Boston Bruins jersey.

"The two jerseys you could buy in Montreal were Canadiens and Toronto. They found a Boston Bruins jersey and they put No. 10 on it for Bill Cowley. That was my big hero. He was a big centerman, as you know. He made more wings than Boeing. From Ottawa. Died a couple of years ago. I visited him.

"There was nobody else around me who followed the Bruins. You're kids, you can't get into much trouble. I used to wear my Boston sweater."

This was Scotty Bowman in his off-ice finest, the raconteur, the historian.

Bowman's street in suburban Verdun was part French-speaking and part-English speaking. He learned both languages, attended a French-speaking school for while. All the kids rooted for the Canadiens and Maroons, except Bowman — and the two kids down the street with their other interests.

"The first game I would have gone to was Canadiens against Maroons,"

Bowman said, "Because my father was a Maroons fan.

"See, when you grew up in Montreal at that time, most of the English were Maroons fans. The French were for the Canadiens ...

"They had what they called in Montreal at the time, they had a rush end. Fifty cents. They called it Millionaires' Row, but it (cost only) 50 cents.

"I remember my dad waited, he used to line up behind the Forum. Obviously in the middle of winter, and he waited for tickets ... Tickets were sold at the corner of Burnside and Atwater. Right on the corner, they had a little wicket there.

Jack Bowman was a soccer player and a blacksmith by trade in Scotland. He emigrated to Canada in 1929. He became a railroad man. In 1930, Bowman's mother, Jean, went to Montreal to marry Jack.

It was from his mother, Jean, that Bowman inherited much of his personality. There were times, it has been reported, that she would respond to weak hands in card games by throwing her cards into the fireplace.

"I grew up on a street, two of the boys became safecrackers," he said once. "They would crack safes. In banks.

"That wasn't the real type of neighborhood it was."

Scotty Bowman did not achieve his boyhood ambition. But his playmates from down the street in Verdun did.

"One ended up in prison in Vancouver," Bowman said, "and the other ended up in the big job (big house) in Boston. They became bank robbers. Armed robbery."

And Bowman collected eight precious Stanley Cup rings.

MEET THE RED WINGS

An inside look at the 1997 Stanley Cup champions

DOUG BROWN

Right wing
Height: 5-10
Weight: 185
Born: June 12, 1964.

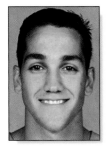

MATHIEU DANDENAULT

Right wing
Height: 5-10
Weight: 185
Born: June 12, 1964.

KRIS DRAPER

Center
Height: 5-11
Weight: 185
Born: May 24, 1971.

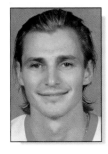

SERGEI FEDOROV

Center
Height: 6-1
Weight: 200
Born: December 13, 1969.

SLAVA FETISOV

Defenseman
Height: 6-1
Weight: 215
Born: April 20, 1958

KEVIN HODSON

Goalie
Height: 6-0
Weight: 178
Born: March 27, 1972

TOMAS HOLMSTROM

Left Wing
Height: 6-0
Weight: 200
Born: January 23, 1973

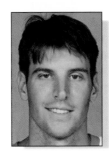

MIKE KNUBLE

Right Wing
Height: 6-3
Weight: 216
Born: July 4, 1972

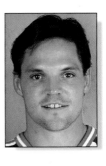

JOE KOCUR

Right Wing
Height: 6-0
Weight: 205
Born: December 21, 1964

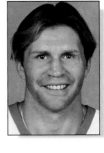

VLADIMIR KONSTANTINOV

Defenseman
Height: 6-0
Weight: 195
Born: March 19, 1967

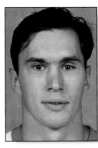

VYACHESLAV KOZLOV

Left Wing
Height: 5-10
Weight: 185
Born: May 3, 1972

MARTIN LAPOINTE

Right Wing
Height: 5-11
Weight: 200
Born: September 12, 1973

IGOR LARIONOV

Center
Height: 5-9
Weight: 170
Born: December 3, 1960

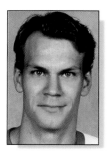

NICKLAS LIDSTROM

Defenseman
Height: 6-2
Weight: 190
Born: April 28, 1970

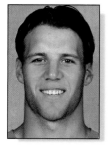

KIRK MALTBY

Left Wing
Height: 6-0
Weight: 185
Born: December 22, 1972

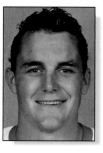

DARREN MCCARTY

Right Wing
Height: 6-1
Weight: 215
Born: April 1, 1972

LARRY MURPHY

Defenseman
Height: 6-2
Weight: 210
Born: March 8, 1961

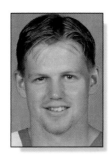

CHRIS OSGOOD

Goalie
Height: 5-11
Weight: 175
Born: November 26, 1972

JAMIE PUSHOR

Defenseman
Height: 6-3
Weight: 210
Born: February 11, 1973

BOB ROUSE

Defenseman
Height: 6-2
Weight: 210
Born: June 18, 1964

TOMAS SANDSTROM

Right Wing
Height: 6-2
Weight: 207
Born: September 4, 1964

BRENDAN SHANAHAN

Left Wing
Height: 6-3
Weight: 218
Born: January 23, 1969

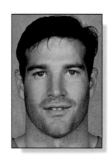

TIM TAYLOR

Center
Height: 6-1
Weight: 190
Born: February 6, 1969

MIKE VERNON

Goalie
Height: 5-10
Weight: 175
Born: February 24, 1963

AARON WARD

Defenseman
Height: 6-1
Weight: 215
Born: January 17, 1973

STEVE YZERMAN

Center
Height: 5-11
Weight: 185
Born: April 9, 1965

SCOTTY BOWMAN

Coach, Director of Player Personnel
Born: September 18, 1933

PHOTOGRAPHERS

Daniel Mears: *6-7, 12, 14, 17, 22, 23, 24, 26-27, 30-31, 34, 35-both, 36-37, 40, 41, 42-both, 43, 50-51, 53, 54, 57, 68-69, 76, 77, 78-79, 87-right, 104, 105, 106-107, 112, 118-119, 120, 123, 128, 140-141, 143, 144-145, 146, 147, 148, 156.*
Alan Lessig: *back cover, 11, 18-19, 21, 25, 28-29, 29, 32-both, 48-49, 55, 66-67, 80, 86, 87-left, 89, 100-101, 102-103, 115, 124, 125, 126, 126-127, 133, 134-135, 137, 153.*
Jack Gruber: *5, 69, 74, 84, 109, 110, 116, 116-117, 138-139, 150.*
Joe DeVera: *4-5, 6.* David Guralnick: *cover, 4, 131.*
Todd McInturf: *4, 6.* Heather Stone: *7.* David Coates: *160.*
The Detroit News file: *90, 92, 95, 96-97, 97, 98, 99, 154.*

PHOTO EDITORS
Amy Kinsella, Steve Haines, Steve Perez, Linda Robak